D0064495

About the Author

Since the year 2000 Hugh Neff and his dawgs from Laughing Eyes Kennel have travelled more than any other musher on the planet competing in 22 thousand mile races and other dog mushing events throughout the world. When it comes to dog mushing, though, day to day living is always the best part of the story.

Photo by Susan Smalley Stevenson

Artist: Pam Lacombe Connell

"This book is dedicated to my boy, Geronimo, and all of the blessed beasts that I have been honored to share the trails with throughout the years."

"So we shall let the reader answer this question for himself. Who is the happier man, he who has braved the storm of life and lived or he who has stayed on shore and merely existed?"

-HST

Tails
of the
Gypsy Musher:

Alaska and Beyond

By Hugh H. Neff
© 2013

Tails of the Gypsy Musher: Alaska and Beyond
© 2013 Hugh Neff
Cover Design: S.G. Sea
Cover Photo: Sweetpea Marie
Back Cover Photo: Susan Smalley Stevenson
"Real Dawgs" Logo Design: S.G.Sea/Running Dog
Designs-AK

ISBN: 978-0-578-13181-8

Laughing Eyes Press
P.O.Box 893
Tok, Alaska
99780

An Alaskan Prayer

*There's a Great Land on my mind, a place I wander
off to from time to time... To see the Future of Man-
kind.
From the highest peaks of Denali, to the shores of the
Bering Sea- How can such beauty truly be?
Keep a sharp eye- wolf, moose, and caribou.
Land of Plentitude.
People?
A few.
Great Almighty let us not destroy this too.
Tell one and all of its endless fall: orange, yellow,
and the reddest of red, immaculate foliage, mosqui-
toes put to bed.
North to the Future, North to the Past. You, are my
true friend, see you soon.
ALLASQ.*

*~The Gypsy Musher
Hugh H. Neff
1992*

Prologue:

He had a Dream

"Hold your breath, make a wish, count to three come with me, and you'll be, in a world of, pure imagination. Take a look, and you'll see, into your imagination.

We'll begin, with a spin, traveling in, the world of my creation, what we'll see, will defy, explanation...

If you want to view paradise,

Simply look around and view it!

Anything you want to, do it!

Wanna change the world?

There's nothing to it. "

-Willy Wonka

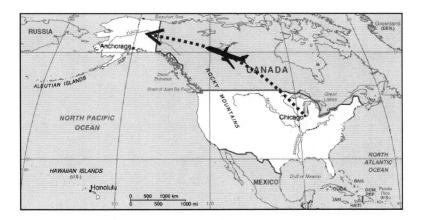

Photo by Nicole Faille

Hi, my name is Walter. Welcome to our Alaskan Adventures! I'd like to introduce you to my buddy, a boy named Hugh. Not the smartest bloke on the block with the prettiest pedigree, just a kid from Chicago searching for his place in history.

Hugh was born in Chattanooga, Tennessee before his family moved to Evanston, Illinois; a Chicago suburb. As a youngster his father, Phil, made sure Hugh had a good work ethic. By the time he was eleven years old, he had a part time job on top of his homework and daily house chores. Hugh loved to come home and play basketball or football with his friends pretending to be like his heroes Walter Payton and a kid named Michael Jordan. Life is never easy though; as a young student from St. Athanasius school he would learn that his mom, Jenny, had died after battling cancer for many years. He was lost without her, but always sought to honor her memory to the best of his abilities.

He first started out working as a paper boy delivering the Chicago Tribune. Everyday he would awaken at five in the morning and hop on his bicycle. So began his daily routine of heading over to the North End News Agency to pick up the few hundred newspapers he would deliver. The news agency supplied him with a wooden newspaper cart that he would push down the streets during the early morning hours, delivering news for all to read that day. Little did he realize, someday in the future, his name and picture would be splashed across its pages.

As he grew older he followed in his older brother Karl's footsteps and became a golf caddy at Westmoreland Country Club in Wilmette, Illinois. Over the years Hugh would become the number one 'Honor Caddy'. He was fortunate enough to carry the golf bags of numerous professional golfers, politicians, as well as one of his favorite actors, Mr. Bill Murray.

A dreamer like most his age, when not working Hugh often borrowed books from his dad's library. The novels he read described far off places where explorers led adventurous lifestyles; his favorite place? Alaska's Greatland...

Hugh was lucky as a kid; his father was wise enough to introduce him to the wondrous ways of the wilderness at a young age. Every summer for a few weeks, he would travel from the noisy streets and bright lights of Chicago, way up north to Lake Killian in Wisconsin. This was where his father's Boy Scout troop had their summer camp, Camp Ma-Ka-Ja-Wan. Hugh was a young 'grubby scout', whom the older kids enjoyed picking on. He was not very tall and rather shy, but he soon learned that, when living in the woods, these traits could be used to his advantage. There was power in learning to be quiet.

Second from left- front row: Future Eagle Scout H.H. Neff

Troop 31 participated every winter in the 'Klondike Derby' where the boy scouts learned how to survive the Windy City's chilly weather, enduring

Lake Michigan's pummeling windstorms. They earned Merit badges too for achieving certain levels of expertise in camping, tying knots, etc. In Hugh's family's garage a few wooden dogsleds had been made by the boys for this winter festival. If he only knew then that one day in the future sleds much like these would be his 'dancing partner' as he dog mushed throughout Alaska.

Often his favorite time of day was actually the night. He felt certain peacefulness in sitting next to a roaring campfire, gazing into the flickering flames, wondering what it really must feel like to be an animal. Along the way Hugh also learned there was power in knowledge and reading. While in scouts he enjoyed learning about the ways of the Native American and their unique society, how the Indians honored the land and tried to live in harmony with it.

Soon he discovered one of his literary heroes, a man named John Muir. John Muir was a writer and naturalist, his books fascinated Hugh's imagination. More than anything Muir was an explorer whose riches were determined by his experiences in life and not by the money he acquired; a fella who would run around Yosemite Park during the middle of an earthquake just to be a part of the fun. Stories such as these intrigued Hugh, he soon discovered other adventurists. Men such as Ernest Shackleton, Roald Amundsen, and Arch-Deacon Hudson Stuck. The Arch-Deacon's novel '10,000 Miles by Dogsled' sent his imagination running wild. Soon all he could think about was playing with dogs up in Alaska's 'Far North.' If he only knew then, that with any dream comes numerous obstacles. The journey he was about to undertake, few could ever imagine. It would never be easy, yet with an unrelenting Passion for life anything is possible…

Some might find it rather strange that a person would seek to live in frigid temperatures for most of the year; especially a city boy who was born in the warm southern climate of Chattanooga, Tennessee. Then again, if you've never felt the freshness of the cool crisp arctic air, there's a vitality one feels at being able to live and prosper, to bloom and grow under such extreme, challenging daily conditions. Sure, life might not always be easy, but numerous rewards were to be discovered along the way. Perseverance would be the key to success. If there is one constant that is certain in life, with human's successes, there are often disappointments too. When things are tough one must never lose hope. All of us have egos, we should be proud of our accomplishments yet wise enough to admit and honor our defeats. For without knowing who you really are, a person can never truly grow…

Over the next decade Hugh traveled all across the United States: camping, fishing, hiking and exploring with his best friends from Troop 31. Seeing new places was what his dream world was all about. Yet there was always something missing, one could see it by the look in his eyes. He was never satisfied; he often stared off into the distance, dreaming of better days to come.

Eventually, after being frugal and saving enough money, Hugh risked it all and set out to chase down his ultimate goal…he was heading north, to the Greatland, to *Alaska*, where his next education would soon begin.

Chapter One:
Struggling to Survive

Eight stars of gold on a field of blue,
Alaska's flag, may it mean to you,
The blue of the sea, the evening sky,
The mountain lakes and the flowers nearby,
The gold of the early sourdough's dreams,
The precious gold of the hills and streams,
The brilliant stars in the northern sky,
The "Bear," the "Dipper," and shining high,
The great North Star with its steady light,
O'er land and sea a beacon bright,
Alaska's flag to Alaskans dear,
The simple flag of a last frontier.

-The Alaska Flag Song

Hi, I am R.E.L. (Rarely Enough Love) I met my master one summer while he was working in the forest just outside of Cor-vallis, Oregon. As you can imagine, my name is a bit unique; as is my master. At first I was a bit wor-ried to be owned by a city boy. After all, the wilds where my ancestors came from are a bit harsher than what humans see on television or in the movies. I was worried, perhaps, that he would take me with him back to Chicago. Fear is usually created by ignorance —not knowing what comes next. When I discovered that we were heading north to romp around and play on one the Earth's grandest playgrounds I was over-joyed with excitement.

Life is never easy; our first few days in Alaska were quite stressful. How would we live? We didn't know anyone, how would we travel? Hugh barely had enough money saved up to feed ourselves for a few weeks. Only time would tell, we had to learn to be positive. With risks, life creates challenges.

After a day's plane flight from the Midwest we landed at Ted Stevens International airport in An-chorage Alaska. We set off on foot, and paws, from there.

We were *Cheechackos*; newcomers to the North. Hugh had overpacked, of course. In fact, many of his belongings were left at the airport never to be seen again. From here on out all he had was a backpack full of clothes and books, a used Schwinn bicycle, and two beautiful dogs to start this new life with—myself and a golden lab named Maverick, the love of his life.

The first few weeks we spent living beside a lake, Westchester Lagoon, underneath some bushes at the end of the Tony Knowles trail. This wasn't exactly living the high life but there was a beauty in struggling to survive. Soon Hugh was able to acquire an old brown Station Wagon so that we could head north in search of his dog mushing dream.

Earlier in the year he had sent a letter to five-time Iditarod champion, Rick Swenson. Hugh was asking for advice about a possible handling position (an assistant to a dog musher). Out of all the famous Iditarod dog mushers, Mr. Swenson was nice enough to send back a reply letter. Unfortunately he informed Hugh that there were no positions available. Swenson mentioned that, when he made it up to Fairbanks, Hugh should go to the local store, Coldspot Feeds, to check for ads on the bulletin board. The six hour drive north to Fairbanks was a harrowing experience for us all.

Considering Hugh had bought the vehicle for just a few hundred dollars it was a miracle we ever made it there.

Every hill was a challenge; could the worn out engine get us to the top? Would the faltering breaks fail us at the bottom? Just a few miles south of Fairbanks, on a hill sitting just above the village of Ester, the car's driveshaft finally gave out. We'd be hitching it from here.

Hitchhiking can be dangerous and difficult enough as it is, but with two dogs I was amazed we got picked up at all. We lucked out and a kind motorist pulled over to give us a lift. It was a tough first night in Fairbanks, not the welcome we had hoped for. By the time the tow truck driver had brought us back to the vehicle, someone had busted a window and stolen some of Hugh's belongings.

That night the Station Wagon sat at Gabe's Junk Yard as we waited for parts to be sent from Anchorage. It wasn't much fun sleeping in a car at temps hovering just above zero; what I remember the most though is the look of amazement in each other's eyes as we stared up at the night sky. At first we thought it was a fireworks show, and then we realized we were seeing the Northern Lights for the first time. Streaks of purple, green, and red flowed back and forth, snaking across the sky. One couldn't help but laugh gazing at the heavens above, for beauty like this was so awe-inspiring it was actually intimidating, and so was the cold.

Fortunately for us, after two weeks of living in the brown Station Wagon along the Tanana River with temps dipping down to twenty below zero, Hugh found work handling for a local sprint dog musher named Bill Mitchell. His chores included feeding, cleaning, caring for, and training Bill's dogs on a daily basis. He so enjoyed the world of dog mushing that within weeks, Hugh was working for two other local mushers as well. He was now helping to care for over two hundred and fifty dogs nearly every day.

This area of Fairbanks was known as Chena Marina. Bill's neighbor was an Athabascan Indian named Curtis Erhart. Curtis grew up in the village of

Tanana, a place we would visit later on down the road.

Hugh's first experience on a sled was in the hills just above Fairbanks. That year, the winter of '95 the snow arrived late. It wasn't until the middle of January that we had a decent amount to play on. Little snow means dangerous trails. It's harder for humans to control dogs if their brakes and snowhooks have nothing to grip down into, so the more snow the better.

Curtis's wife Shannon asked Hugh to accompany her on a run along Old Murphy Dome Road. As the dog team flew down the road, Hugh held on for dear life. He wasn't in control. He was on the second, trailing sled, which was hooked by a cable wire to Shannon's sled directly in front of him; she was in charge of things. As they turned around on their short, hour long run, Hugh's sled careened into a snow embankment and he was flipped off; his shoulder slamming into the road's hard surface.

All Hugh could do was watch as Shannon and the fired up sixteen dog team flew back to the dog truck.

Over the next few hours—as he walked back, embarrassed by his first performance, his shoulder throbbing in pain—he realized that sometimes in life, things aren't as easy as they seem.

Through trials and tribulations, Hugh slowly evolved as a dog musher. Each month he would acquire a new pup to raise in exchange for cleaning his neighbor, Ramey's, dog yard. First there was Marcellus, then June Mari. Within a few months, Laughing Eyes Kennel was transforming from a dream into reality.

In some parts of Alaska there are four dogs to every human. A wise newcomer to the North learns to be cautious when acquiring animals. Is there a reason this dog is being offered to me? The dogs of Alaska aren't your typical household pet, their energy is often limitless. To be a real dog musher, one must learn that it isn't just about what you own, but how you care for it. Husky's deserve and require lots of attention. The more you take care if them, the more they learn to take care of you. We are not just master and servant. On the trail we are of one spirit.

With little money to his name, Hugh learned to be frugal. After all, caring for a dozen dawgs isn't exactly cheap. He never made any money as a handler, only room and board. Soon he would find odd jobs, to keep the dream alive. Whether it be cleaning restrooms, washing dishes, selling firewood or changing out truck tires, his passion for dog mushing lead him to do whatever it would take.

With a will there would be a way.

Chapter Two:
Our Canine Community

"It's fun to have fun, but you have to know how."

-Dr.Suess

Princess and her puppies　　　　*Photo by Nicole Faille*

Photo by Nicole Faille

How ya doing? My name is Stevie Ray and I'm the toughest pup around! If you want to be a real dawg, one must be willing to play any position on the team. Up in lead or in the wheel, give it your all, and learn to make your effort always real. My master likes to keep me back towards the sled when we're going real fast because I'm not the speediest fella. If the snow gets deep however, put me up in lead and I will get you through those tough times on the trail.

Mother Nature always offers daily challenges, whether it be drifted snow or overflow. Yet there is a sense of harmony living as one with the earth; taking what is offered and giving it to others to watch them grow.

We are more than just a dog yard or kennel; Laughing Eyes is a canine community. Just imagine living every day with fifty other furry friends to play with! In some respects our dog yard is Hugh's garden; he just wants us to be as healthy as possible. For hours twice a day every day, he is out there with a shovel in one hand and a poop bucket in the other, making sure everything is nice and neat. He might be known as "Huge Mess" but our dog yard certainly isn't. There are numerous reasons why he keeps it clean, not only for my well being but for the well being of all our community. Disease tends to spread in places that aren't kept clean. Learning to care for our surroundings is the best way to honor this treasure called life. Fortunately for us, our caretakers are kind and wise enough to spend quality time with us; not only feeding and cleaning up for all of the pooches, but most importantly — BONDING with us! They realize that it's the cohesiveness of all of our behaviors that promises a healthier fur-ball society; day in, day out. Whether we are four months, four years, or fourteen, our value to one another as a community will always be appreciated.

Photo by Nicole Faille

With fifty dogs in the yard, not everybody is going to like each other. That's just the way this world is. Some dawgs are kept away from their adversaries. They aren't necessarily mean; they are just trying to assert their dominance instinctively. Often brothers from the same litter will get into skirmishes, surging at each other like sumo wrestlers as they fight over a nearby bone. Unfortunately some dawgs can become jealous of others when they receive too much human attention and are treated more like pets. This jealousy can lead to teeth being bared as warning signs. Our community is constantly being rotated around like musical chairs according to social structure, and whatever brings about the greatest peace and harmony. With dozens of wild and energized pooches, human caretakers must provide structure. Not only in how we are placed together in a team but our housing as well. In some parts of the world folks who own large numbers of dogs must have them kept in pens. In Alaska, either dog pens or tethering is acceptable. The funny thing is, some folks deem tethering to be "deplorable" but I tell you what—in our yard, nine times out of ten, your typical pooch would rather be out in the yard with the rest of the main racing Dawgs then in a pen staring out through a fence. Sure, pups, gals in heat, and some old timers might need the security of those four walls but for most of us it's all about being out there with the rest of the team seeing life! To evolve we all need to learn to get along to the best of our abilities, the alternative would not be as enjoyable. Whichever way one chooses to care for their loved ones day to day loving and exercise are what it's really all about. Who feels like howling?

There are always a few elder statesmen sauntering about keeping an eye on the rest of us. Around the dog yard, Walter is in charge. Along with Delilah, Jewel, and a few other chosen team captains who wander around our canine community each day making sure that everyone is getting along. The puppies have their pen, the retired dawgs do too, though we'd prefer to hang out with our racing buddies; especially our master Hugh. He's not the most normal human in the world; he's constantly muttering to himself, trying to remember all there is to do. Every day after Hugh has had his morning coffee we watch as he runs around in circles performing chores. Some folks think that we dawgs work for him however our little secret is that he is actually our man servant; cooking our grub two or three times each day, cleaning the yard, and taking us out for exercise on a regular basis.

Each morning before the sun comes up water must be hauled in five gallon buckets to help prepare the day's meals. In colder weather, a fire must be made in order to warm up the dogs stew. Yet for every chore that must be done, there are rewards of gratification. After every meal, my buddies and I let out a chorus of howls, thanking our caretaker for the fine meal we have enjoyed. It might be fish, or moose, store bought meats, or what have you. The amount of effort one gives to their dogs is shown in the happiness and well being of each individual dog's character.

A wise dog musher realizes that it's the consistent love and respect for their dawgs which makes them a winner in the end. The bonds shared between our canine companions create an overall happiness, an 'aura' that is enjoyable to be a part of. Crazy things can happen though; we are just like a big classroom of furry kids after all.

You had better be careful around

Photo by Nicole Faille

feeding time with dozens of dawgs running around their houses screaming for chow. The only time it gets louder is if we are hollering to be hooked up on a run.

As pups we're taught how to act properly in the team by an older dawg who already 'knows the ropes'. Younger pups will be teamed up in pens to learn from the older pooches about trail etiquette. While most humans are always telling their dogs what to do, wise mushers realize we learn our habits by watching what others do. Hopefully we pick up on their better traits if we're seeking to become good leaders in the future out on the trail.

Photo by Nicole Faille

Brothers and sisters often share dog pens as well so they can play with their puppyhood buddies as much as possible. Typically we snuggle up together in houses that are within our area. Our playground, when not romping out on the trails, is our pens in the warmer summer months. Our 'Romper room' is big enough to run around and play in but not too large that we are prone to starting trouble. We must always have an eye kept on us—kids can get pretty pumped up with all the good meat, fish, and kibble we like to chow down on! Having older dogs to follow around helps us to learn, and ya know what? I think we keep our canine 'elders' happier too. After all, it's never too late to have an enjoyable child-hood.

Photo by Nicole Faille

In the wintertime, once the lakes and rivers freeze up, our master's chores increase with the cold. Now he has to break open a hole through thick ice, often three or four feet deep. Sometimes a chainsaw will work but often a pick axe might be needed. Mushers rarely get cold around their kennels; they stay warm by working for us Dawgs all the time. Five gallon buckets of water must be carried from the lake to the cooker. Once a raging fire is going fish, fat and other food will be added to the pot to create a delectable doggie stew. Making sure to eat good food ensures that you will have a healthy body, which helps to create a healthy mind.

Once feeding time commences the dog yard becomes more structured as we are all led back to our proper houses and are secured safely. There's a sense of excitement in the air as the fresh aroma of our next meal permeates through the air. It builds up into a frenzy of noise as dozens of hungry fur-balls circle their houses. Chow time is but a minute or two away. Each of us pooches is given a few scoops to gobble down. Most of us are in such a hurry to eat that our tasty meals disappear before we even realize it. Once all of us have been fed, Hugh will walk back through the dog yard to make sure that everyone has a healthy appetite and no one is feeling sluggish or sick.

Ellsworth, Tolliver, and Tyler   *Photo by Nicole Faille*

The greatest compliment we ever received was from another musher's wife who told Hugh that his dogs were so "Elegant." For some reason he felt humbled by compliments such as this. June Mari, Delilah, Annie, and I have always known we were born to good pedigree, but daily grooming ensures over all beauty in the long run.

For us dawgs here at Laughing Eyes Kennel the world revolves around our canine community. Just like in school we have our cliques of friends that like to hang out together. Annie's Army has their playground pen to play in, of course; the pups need to be kept to themselves. Prancing around in another area are Omen's offspring. Scattered about in between are various older retired dawgs who spend most of their time chillin' out and enjoying the view.

We hear that other humans think dawg mushers are a little goofy in the head because of all the work they have to do each day in order to take care of us properly. Why not just use a snow machine or four-wheeler? Most people can't understand the incredible feeling of traveling across a mountain range or wide open river in the silence of the North. When all one hears is the panting of our breath and the hiss of the sleds runners. Sometimes in life the most beautiful thing to listen to is pure silence.

Sure it's fun being out on the trail; yet, sometimes travelling the same route all the time can be a little bit tedious. Maybe my back feels a bit sore, or pulling the sled feels more like a chore.

At times like these the Gypsy Musher can sense our team's boredom with doing the same old thing. That's when it's time to load up in the truck and explore new areas. Hugh realized when this dream began that the key to life was to 'Never Stop Exploring'; not only the world around you but the world within you. Every time he's out in the dog yard hooking up a team he's mixing and matching us, seeing who gets along with whom, realizing it's not about who the stars are, but what's best for team unity. One learns in this world there are a lot of pretty people but true beauty comes from the heart. Sure we get pampered a lot, and I, of course, love lying on the couch. Yet, to be real, never take how lucky you are for granted. Seeing the positive in any situation helps one to keep growing and getting better in the long run. I enjoy the comforts of civilization but for the most part I am an outside dawg--a true 'Wilderness Warrior".

During the fall season younger dawgs with too much energy will be harnessed up for the first time and shown the ways of the trail, each yearling will be placed next to an older pooch that will teach them the ropes. Not only how to pull, which to a Husky comes quite naturally, but more importantly the elder dawgs teach us how to better conserve our energy so that it may last for the longer runs. It's easy for anyone to be a loud cheerleader before the game begins, but when the contest is on the line at the very end of the game it's the true players whose talents rise to the occasion.

It's never a good idea to put two young pups in a team next to each other. Whenever this happens one of them usually needs a time out afterwards as they like to nip and play with each other instead of concentrating on learning the day's lesson. If there is a troublemaker in the group we call them an alligator; someone who likes to bite and bark at everyone else. Pups like these tend to not get run as much; their actions make it harder on everyone in the long run. That's why it is smart to be quiet, listen and learn from your elders. Usually they are not trying to show off how smart they are, but are helping the younger fur balls learn to avoid making mistakes that they once did. Maybe it's being too hyper which causes you to tire quicker, or perhaps viewing their steady gait, which conserves energy. I love hanging out with older folks, they are a fountain of information that I can use to become smarter and stronger! Real dawgs know how to get along.

When hooking up a team the dog yard's emotions are even louder than at feeding time, we're all swirling around in circles begging to be picked to go on the next run. "Over here! Pick me! It's my turn!" Sixteen dawgs hooting and hollering all at once ready to charge on down the trail. It's too early in the season to use a dogsled just yet, there's no snow on the ground so we are forced to use a four-wheeler.

Heading out of the dawg yard we suddenly become silent, a mushing machine in motion as we march along as one. Every so often we will stop to take a breather, and perhaps a quick potty break. Within seconds of resting, there's usually one goofball, yipping and yapping, wanting to get goin' again. Our master waits though, for in dog mushing, as well as many other things, patience is a virtue.

Besides, the barking of the dawgs is also a warning to our forest dwelling friends of our imminent arrival. "Beware the rest of you creatures out there, we're coming though, better watch out! It's us dawgs again…and Hugh."

At such an early age our bodies aren't developed enough to go very far. We're learning from experience what is expected of us, how to be proper team members. There are no show-offs in this group. We learn to work together as one; a single trouble maker amongst us can ruin all of the fun.

Each of us gets a chance to run up in lead, to give it our best shot. Sure we might not make the main team until we get a little bit older, but who knows? Sooner or later we might be there to save the day when times get tough.

Nathan   *Photo by Tamra Reynolds*

Everyday day life at fifty below can lead to some interesting situations at times. Each year the eastern Interior area around Tok receives some of the coldest weather in Alaska. Temps can even dip down to sixty below — we prefer just for a few days but ya never know — we might be living in a freezer for *weeks* at a time. Life is difficult for everyone whether they be wolves, moose, us dawgs, or our human counter-parts. Thankfully our caretakers are wise enough to place plenty of straw in our houses for us to stay com-fortable and warm. Some of the dogs with less fur are brought inside or else we snuggle up with our buddies, sharing each other's warmth. The frigid air is dangerous as well; we are more likely to just run around the yard for exercise than train on any extended runs. Heck, most of the time our human friends are worried about keeping all of their conveniences in proper working order.

The use of firewood for heating homes can double. Cutting up logs at forty below is easier but everything is fairly brittle in these temps and even steel can break. How cold is it? Well, the old saying is that you can take a bucket of water and throw it in the air — by the time the water reaches the ground it's already becoming ice. People's homes are their safety nests in these dangerous conditions. Pipes can burst quite easily. Having no access to water is not good when there are dozens of dogs needing to be hydrated properly. Cell phones and other gadgets are not of much use either; their batteries freeze solid in *minutes*.

The strangest story I ever heard happened a few years ago in the town of Delta Junction just west of here. Hugh was hauling a team to Fairbanks for their vet checks before the Yukon Quest race. He stopped at a fuel station to fill up his tank, which is wise when temps are *so* cold. As he placed the nozzle and began fueling his vehicle the hose cracked open and burst with diesel pouring all over the parking lot. Thankfully workers were there to make sure it was shut off immediately.

At forty below truck tires freeze up, resembling somewhat square blocks rather than circular wheels. Engines must be plugged in at night so oil and batteries don't freeze too.

There's a reason some humans find dogs more dependable. We might be ornery at times and cost a lot to feed but when Mother Nature unleashes her mighty wrath we'll get ya where you need to go. Haste makes waste, learning to abide by Mother Nature's rules using caution creates a safer trail in the long run. Dressing properly with good feet protection, fur for our private parts, hands, and head helps too. Hoping for the best but preparing for the worst is our motto out on the trail when dealing with difficult weather conditions. Staying positive and not stressing is important as well—no matter what the temp might be consistency, having good habits, is our greatest Ally!

Chapter three:
Nuchalawoya –
Living amongst our Native Athabascan Friends

"Give whatever you got and you'll get in return something better than what you give. You believe that? You got to share. That's true. That's the old Indian way. That's what we were taught."
~Chief Peter John
1900-2003

Erhart Family

Lester Erhart is one of the toughest men I have ever known, a true Dog-Man. There's a reason why we Erhart dogs are some of the finest around! To us he is the 'godfather' of Tanana. Twice the age of most of the younger folks, Lester tends to put in double the amount of work as other people do on a daily basis. We're not talking paperwork either; he doesn't just put on a tie and sit at a desk every day. Lester is an Athabascan elder; he's been hunting, fishing, or collecting wood nearly everyday of his life. As a hobby, he's also a gifted violinist. In Alaska they call musicians like him 'Athabascan fiddlers.'

Every weekend family and friends gather at his home along the Yukon River to listen to his country music with native soul. Along with his band, Lester has brought a lot of happiness to his people through the art of singing, showing others how to dance the night away.

Running dawgs has been what he and his family have been about for decades as well. Whether it be for sprint mushing or long distance adventures, Yukon River sled dogs are some of the finest around.

My momma, Colby, often told me stories of what it was like to live in Tanana, though I was barely old enough to remember. "It's a windswept place in

Alaska's interior where day to day living is a tough existence."

Each year Lester and his sons, Curtis, Chuckie, Oodie, John, Ronnie, and Carl, participate not only in the two famous sprint races—the Fur Rendezvous in Anchorage, as well as the North American championships in Fairbanks—but numerous other smaller village races too. Some of the dogs that aren't fast enough will be sold to long-distance mushers who compete in a different style of racing that travels at a different pace and is more about consistent strength than overall speed.

Anvik, Alaska   *Photo by Stephen Nowers*

The natives call Tanana by the name Nuchala-woya, which means 'where the rivers meet'. Just take a look at a map of Alaska, this village of six-hundred people lies directly in the middle of the Greatland. It's expensive to be a musher in these parts. With air freight, each bag of dog food costs about ten dollars extra. The natives often harvest fish called Chum Salmon from the Yukon River with their fish wheels to help feed their dogs. Coming from Chicago it must have felt quite strange for Hugh to live in such a unique and remote environment, yet he and his native friends also had many things in common; their love of the dogs as well as a deep rooted reverence for 'Indian Country'.

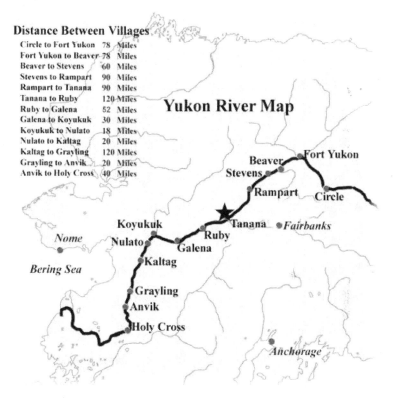

Distance Between Villages

Circle to Fort Yukon	78 Miles
Fort Yukon to Beaver	78 Miles
Beaver to Stevens	60 Miles
Stevens to Rampart	90 Miles
Rampart to Tanana	90 Miles
Tanana to Ruby	120 Miles
Ruby to Galena	52 Miles
Galena to Koyukuk	30 Miles
Koyukuk to Nulato	18 Miles
Nulato to Kaltag	20 Miles
Kaltag to Grayling	120 Miles
Grayling to Anvik	20 Miles
Anvik to Holy Cross	40 Miles

Yukon River Map

Lester would often take Hugh out in the wilderness in his sled basket and teach him the ways of arctic survival, "Always remember when going down the trail, keep an eye out for dead trees, you never know when you will need to start a fire in an emergency situation."

Lester occasionally gave Hugh younger dogs to help train them up at a slower pace that they could handle. The only problem was, once the dogs were looking real good and Hugh was ready to take them to one of his races. Lester would find someone looking to buy a dog. One week he'd be training a future leader, the next week Hugh would be racing against them!

There's much more to dog mushing than just racing but training is what Hugh really enjoys the most. Watching how the youngster develops, seeing their personalities mature through time. Usually this is accomplished by going on overnight camping trips.

Being a newcomer to this area Hugh was still quite the Greenhorn; when out on the trails of Alaska's unforgiving wilderness, one must proceed with caution. This was something his 'city boy ways' didn't allow for at times.

In January of 1999 we set out from Tanana heading toward Manley. From Manley we were to hitch a ride into Fairbanks so that we could participate in the Fireplug race. Unlike most dog mushing events, in many parts of "Bush" Alaska the trails are not marked very well—sometimes not at all. The first twenty miles out of Tanana could be rather challenging at times. Heading down Hay Slough one winter, just south of Tanana, we had to plow through two feet of open water for a few hours at fifty below. By the time we got home Hugh looked like a frozen tin man. This year, however, the trail was decent. As we reached the end of the creek, we crossed over a few ponds before the dog team came to Fish Lake.

The trail winds its way nearly five miles across this mammoth body of water. Unfortunately that season the tenacious winds had knocked down all the trail markers. We would have to find the portage on the other side that would lead us the rest of the way to Manley on our own.

At around four in the afternoon, as the sun set to the west, we slowly crept across the slick icy surface. Keeping an eye out for any sign of snow machine tracks, we continued on. Half-an-hour later, as darkness finally ensued, the trail gradually disappeared. Things were looking bleak as we eventually made it to the other side, wallowing through a few feet of fresh snow. If there was a trail to be found, it would not be tonight, for our energy was exhausted and our spirits were weak.

Photo by Svein Kartvedt

Setting the snowhook and parking the team safely, Hugh set out to seek firewood to build a fire for warmth in the forty below temperatures. Before we left Tanana Lester had warned Hugh about wolf sightings in the general area, thus his nerves were on high alert. Add in the fact that he was a bewildered city boy on his first major journey alone and he would be lucky to get a blink of sleep. He sat awake for awhile worrying for his own well being, but eventually he did doze off with some of the dogs curled around his sleeping bag. An hour had passed before he was suddenly startled from his dream world. Hugh had miscalculated the size of his fire and his sleeping bag was now aflame, melting down by his feet! He quickly rolled in the snow to put out the blaze.

This was going to be a *long* night!

Having fur ourselves, we all sat back and chuckled at this silly boy's behavior.

Manley Hot Springs   *Photo by Nicole Faille*

The following morning we finally discovered the portage trail and set off towards Manley Hot Springs. A few moments later there was a noise coming towards us from the other side of the Lake. It was a snow machine! A search party had been sent out to look for the 'lost' musher. It was Hugh's buddies

Dougie, Drew, and Dozer from Tanana. They shared some coffee and salmon strips with him as he recounted his long night of restlessness. Glancing back at their snow machine he noticed there was a sled being dragged behind it. He inquired as to what it was for. They replied," Oh that? That's a body bag, Ya know, just in case..."

Stories like this are not uncommon in the far north; it's a vast wilderness, but in many respects, it's one large village. Folks are always looking out for one another. You never know when it might be time for you to help a person in need or to have someone lend you a hand.

Chapter Four:

Animal Encounters

"In every walk with nature one receives far more than he seeks."

-John Muir

Artist: Pam Lacombe Connell

The following spring Laughing Eyes Kennel decided to move on from Tanana, travelling nearly a hundred miles upriver to the village of Nenana, which resides at the confluence of the Tanana and Nenana rivers adjacent to the Parks Highway. Every spring this village has a contest to see when a large black and white striped wooden tripod will fall into the Tanana River, signaling the start of the boating season. Fortunately for Hugh we arrived in Nenana when all the rivers and lakes were frozen. There would still be time to explore the new area by dogsled. Many champion mushers have lived and trained in these parts: Rick and Dick Mackey, Charlie Boulding, and Gerald Riley, just to name a few.

His favorite day of the week to run was always early on a Sunday morning, Hugh called this "going to church", a time to worship and give praise to the Greatland with which he was so in love. On one such occasion, we were heading down the trail about an hour outside of town. The trail ran along a huge swath of spruce trees next to the power line just north of Nenana. There was a parallel trail just a few hundred feet to the left of us. In the early morning darkness all of the Dawgs' eyes and ears instinctively alerted us to the fact that we were not alone. Within seconds a large momma moose, weighing in at over half a ton, was flying towards the team.

Her ferocious glaring eyes, nearly the size of an egg in diameter, stared down upon us and steam billowed from her nostrils in the early morning's sub zero temperatures. We could tell she was not very happy; her massive body bristled with aggression. We were in trouble now!

Looking directly behind her we noticed that she was protecting her young calf. Immediately our team gee'd over to the right and onto a different trail as we headed south just behind Iditarod champion Dick Mackey's house. The calf and mother were now racing us as they ran directly next to us on the parallel trail. It seemed as though this scene went on for hours though it lasted only ten or fifteen minutes. Now I've been in a lot of races before and I have to tell you, our team of dawgs was flying; over twenty miles per hour, which is pretty fast for us. The amazing part was that calf and mother left us in the dust as if we had the speed of a turtle. We sure were glad they did! By the time we got back to the house safely, I think our master's prayers had been answered for that day. As far as moose encounters go, though, that was nothing compared to what happened before our first Yukon Quest race. I will let my friend, Marcellus, tell you about it. He was in the lead for that harrowing encounter.

Just before our first Yukon Quest race started in February of 2000 our team was training up by Murphy Dome, in Fairbanks. We were performing a ten mile 'fun run' a few days before the long journey was to begin. With only a few minutes left in our run, lightning struck. Rounding a bend in the trail we noticed a giant bull moose awaiting our arrival. Its stomach was roughly the height of my master's head and this ornery critter did not seem to be in any hurry to move out of our way. It was much easier for the heavy set animal to walk on our hard packed trails than the four or five feet of fluffy soft snow that lay next to him.

Not knowing what to do, Hugh stopped his sled, slamming the snowhook into the ground. Within seconds my teammates and I were roaring our disdain at the moose with all of our energy; we wanted to get home for some chow!

The moose replied by heading straight towards us at a slow gallop, heading straight for Hugh. He instinctively jumped off the back of the sled, screaming out, "GO HOME MARCELLUS, GET OUT OF HERE NOW!"

Immediately my doggy cohorts and I took off, running for our lives. With all of our might we ripped the snowhook out of the trail and flew off towards safety; the cabin!

Unfortunately for the moose, as we bolted down the trail its hoof became entangled in the sled causing this behemoth of a beast to fall sideways, flattening the wooden sled into pieces. As we dragged this enraged animal a few hundred feet life was just a big ball of confusion. Luckily, as the team descended down the hill, a sharp turn in the trail helped to flip our woodland friend loose from the sled. Last time we saw that big fella he was flying for the freedom of the forest.

I think the whole experience might have 'shaken' him up a bit.

Moments later we arrived at our buddy Rich's cabin, he was kind enough to secure the team and give us each some beaver broth as a reward for our efforts. It was such a tasty treat that by the time Hugh arrived a half hour later we barely even noticed his return. As they say, if you want a dog to love ya, you better feed them well!

The next night—before our first big race, the Yukon Quest, was to begin—Hugh and his buddy Rich would stay up into the wee hours of the morning, putting the Percy Dyke sled back together again.

As for the moose?

I'm sure he's still having nightmares about our encounter.

The moose encounter was a crazy experience. When you travel as much as we do one is bound to see lots of interesting sights as well as have numerous encounters with Mother Nature's forest dwellers. Moose can be dangerous, yet that was nothing compared to what a dawg by the name of Deyaah once experienced.

Now Deyaah wasn't a sled dog like the rest of us, in fact she was what we dawgs call a 'village animal'. I'll always remember the first day she came into our lives. We were on a training run heading back to Fairbanks from Minto. About ten miles outside of this small village, Hugh stopped the team as he glanced down the trail behind us. We noticed a black fur-ball running towards us, nearly a half a mile away. At first we were worried that it might be a rabid wolf but soon we could tell by its prance that is was just a puppy, lost and looking for company.

Hugh scooped up the pup once she became tired and placed her in the sled bag. Arriving home the next day Hugh called his friend Lloyd Charlie in Minto explaining the situation. Lloyd replied, "Well you better just keep her; she obviously loves you!"

Photo by Nicole Faille

Hugh named Deyaah after the village of Minto. She was one of the fastest dogs in our kennel for years; her only problem was she preferred to run around loose chasing animals instead of pulling a sled like the rest. Deyaah was more of a Labrador mix than a husky; she instinctively had no desire to pull like we do.

Typically we ran training runs that consisted of thirty miles at a time, whether it be one or two training runs a day, Hugh would always be our musher back on the sled's runners guiding us down the trail. Deyaah would come along too, running loose in front of the team. In some respects she was the expedition's main leader preparing a safe passage on the trail before us, making sure there were no moose in our way.

The wildest experience she ever encountered happened a few miles to the east of Coldfoot, Alaska, in the mountains known as the Brooks Range.

The dog team had just crossed over Myrtle creek when I suddenly noticed an unfamiliar scent in the air. Glancing to the sides of the trail I noticed large paw prints everywhere. No, this wasn't another moose to mess with. This was our mortal enemy, Canis Lupus; the wolf.

Up in the far North they are known as the 'Lords of the Forest'. Wolves are rarely seen, they are wise enough to hide from others and smart enough to team up while hunting. Unfortunately for us, on today's menu, we were considered the prey. That morning temps were in the negative twenties. Lil' did we realize, within the next minutes, Deyaah would be fighting and fleeing for her life. I guess we should let her describe what happened next.

My master and the dog team were just a few hundred feet in front of me as I continued on down the trail accelerating my pace; I knew I was being watched. It was time to skedaddle...the hunt had begun.

Glancing back I could see a ghostly shadow creeping closer. A mile later, I thankfully caught up next to my master's sled, barking all the while. He looked at me in disbelief, wondering what all the yapping was about. I wasn't about to slow down and explain things as I flew off in front of the dog team in search of safety. Hugh swerved around finally realizing that the wolf was now less than fifty feet behind him and was coming on strong.

Quickly he stopped the team securing the snowhook into the frozen earth. The wolf instantaneously veered from the trail choosing to hide behind some bushes. We were all wide awake and on high alert now! Coming to his senses, Hugh placed me inside his sled bag and out of harms way. Turning the team around we cruised back heading for Coldfoot at a speed any famous sprint mushing team would have been proud of. Those ten miles felt like an eternity for me. The pumped up fourteen-dog team was flying, yet the wolf stayed with us easily, only a few yards behind the frantic, squeamish squad. With its haunting yellow eyes, this predator seemed to flow over the snow as if it were a ghost. Its massive paws and long gangly body allowed it to barely sink into the snow compared to the rest of us dawgs. We would later find out this wolf had rabies, which causes an animal's brain to go crazy. It was not just hungry; most critters of the north would be afraid of a human but not this sick animal.

Just outside of Coldfoot we came upon a small stream about a hundred feet in width. We plunged our way through its icy cold water not realizing we had created our own freedom. The wolf had stopped on the other side of the creek. It would pursue us no further, suddenly our momentum ceased as well. All of the dawgs looked back at Hugh with disbelief, why had he stopped the sled? He was now rummaging through his pockets, what was he looking for? The camera's flash helped us to realize that he was only being the professional tourist and taking a picture. After all how often does a human get chased by a wolf these days?

As far as race experiences that have involved wildlife, Walter probably remembers this next moment the most...

Photo by Al Grillo/AP

It happened in one of the shorter races called the Cantwell Classic. It was a two hundred mile event that started in Cantwell and went down the Denali Highway, just to the east of Denali National Park. This encounter occurred with only fifty miles left in the race. Our team was doing quite well; we were in 5th place out of a few dozen teams.

Nearing the Big-Su River we were just a few miles away from the final checkpoint. The trail on this section was long and straight—one could see for miles.

All of our ears perked up, as we could hear a small rodent crossing the trail just up ahead. Coming closer to this small black blob, Hugh slammed his foot on the sled's break. He realized that it was best not to mess with this critter, for it was the mighty porcupine. 'Lil' Porky' would decide when we were allowed to move again. Fifteen minutes passed and finally the porky had disappeared off into the bushes away from the trail. We resumed our march to the nearby checkpoint.

For some reason my brother Watson and I instinctively followed the porky's smell away from the trail and into the bushes. I had never met one of these creatures before; I was intrigued to see what they were all about.

To sum up the next few minutes of my life I would say, "Ouch, the pain!"

There is nothing like having porcupine quills stuck into your face, snout and paws. I blame it on the porcupine, but to be honest, we were the ones attacking it. He was just defending himself.

Having assessed the situation Hugh realized that this was a major emergency. My brother Watson and I were both in a lot of pain and needed medical attention A.S.A.P. After securing us in the sled, the team carried us to the checkpoint ten minutes later.

Dr. Jane and the Veterinarians were kind enough to care for us and pull the quills out. They determined that I would no longer be able to participate in the race. My brother Watson was lucky; he only had a few quills in his snout. Once they pulled them out he was allowed to continue on. (I would heal up eventually after being driven back to the starting line via snow machine.) For the remaining fifty miles the team was on cruise control, finishing in second place overall. Spectators at the event said they could tell by watching Watson that he wasn't just racing. For the final fifty miles of the trail he was up in lead constantly searching both sides of the trail hunting for more porcupines.

Photo by Sam Harrell

The greatest trophies of any race are the mesmerizing experiences seen on the trail. Most mushers are in a hurry to make it to the finish line, whereas the experienced souls realize it's the journey which is the greatest treasure of all; climbing thousands of feet to witness views that few human eyes have ever encountered. The opportunity to look out over valleys that stretch dozens of miles in every direction is a heavenly view to enjoy. The descent down the summit can be a bit more nerve wracking though, as one worries for the safety of their team members; caution is a must on this roller coaster ride which stretches out for days on end. Protecting one's dogs is always #1 on the list, especially when animals are encountered. The more one travels through the wilderness the greater the odds of running into critters along the way, especially if they are up near the front of the pack.

Just a few months ago, during the Kobuk 440 race up in Kotzebue, we experienced one of these treasured animal encounters that were an amazing "trophy" to witness.

Towards the end of the Kobuk 440 with less than a hundred miles left, our team became a part of another race which we had no intentions of winning.

Leaving the Eskimo village of Selawik, dog teams travel a few hours over the ice before entering a pass which, once summited, drops down into the final checkpoint — the village of Noorvik. As we crept up through the hills my mind was exhausted, groggy from days without sleep. George and I were pretty tired too as we had just been in Norway racing a few weeks earlier. It had been a *long* racing season. "Almost done for the year kids, you're doing good!"

It was ten o'clock at night as the northern arctic skies slowly darkened. It being the middle of April, this far north true darkness was becoming scarce. Looking off to the left I noticed movement, there was a caribou watching us. No, wait...there's another one...two, three, four...thirteen of them! Holy cow!

Fortunately the trail veered to the right, away from all of the foraging critters; the last thing we want is to get involved with that crowd. Glancing back, I noticed that the caribou were now marching in a single file line up the hill and in our direction. "C'mon George, let's go guys, let's get out of here!"

The contest was just beginning. As we accelerated our pace it must have spooked the herd, for suddenly they all started running too. Known as a rather timid animal, I was confused by their actions—but not in the mood to go over and interview the head caribou as to why they were acting in such a way.

Photo by Nicole Faille

A few minutes later and we were now neck and neck, my team of trail weary pooches versus thirteen caribou, still in single file just above us on the hill heading towards Noorvik. Moments such as this move in slow motion, minutes feel like hours, time stands still.

Our teams were parallel to each other, everyone's senses were on overdrive, and I could not help but start giggling at our team's latest rival. "You have got to be kidding me—unreal!"

I wasn't afraid, perhaps a bit nervous but experiences like this are what we *live* for. These eyes have seen quite a lot throughout the years but nothing has brought me so in touch with Mother Nature's exquisite children as this decisive moment. The race was on. Who would win? Well, if I was a betting dog the odds would be heavily on the fresh, well fed Caribou, who within seconds went from a few feet away, to way up on the hill a quarter mile in front of us. Those critters were cruising!

Photo by S.G.Sea

For some unknown reason Hugh instinctively started to whistle up the team, "We can do better than this, kids—they're leaving us in the dust." And then it happened; all thirteen curious Caribou stopped and intently stared at us as we wandered our way over the twisty trail and away from their safe haven. For those final few minutes we, the dogs and musher, were the "ZOO" being analyzed by our new found friends.

Some humans will tell you that animals are not smart, that their brains are not quite as 'good' as people brains. Our master often wonders though, who are we to judge them — is it all about how big your head is, or if you are putting your brain to good use? We bid adieu to our forest dweller friends as the lights of the village came into view, no matter how large the purse or size of the trophy cherished moments becoming one with the dog team, the Earth and her natural wilderness inhabitants are what our simple city boy's dream is all about. Unreal, unreal.

"Y'all having fun yet kidzzz?"

Chapter Five:

Frozen Foot Neff of the North

"Is it raining? Is it snowing? Is a hurricane a-blowing? Not a speck of light is showing, so the danger must be growing."

-Willy Wonka

Photo by Dick Mackey

Photo by Nicole Faille

Sometimes in life you have to make decisions in order to simply survive. I don't think our master ever planned on working at Alaska's farthest northern truck stop in the garage as a tire-boy, yet where there's a will there's a way to make things happen despite not having much money to one's name. When the opportunity to train dogs for the winter in Coldfoot arose, Hugh packed up our belongings in his old beat up pickup truck and headed north.

There are not too many dog mushing folks who train this far north, a six hour drive up the Dalton Highway, from Fairbanks.

The Dalton Highway is the main supply road for the Prudhoe Bay oil fields up near Barrow, at the farthest north tip of Alaska. Few humans even live in this area. It was a tough existence but Hugh had a paying job and free leftovers from the buffet line to help feed his dogs. I'd definitely rather eat Eggs Benedict over dog kibble any day of the week. He was the kid in the garage who fixed flat tires on the massive semi trucks that were hauling supplies north.

Hugh loved to travel by dog team up in the valleys of the Brooks Range. Whether it be the *Gates of the Arctic National Park* or heading down the trail to visit his friends at Chandalar Lake, some seventy miles east of Coldfoot; the beauty of the far north was mesmerizing. The Brooks Range offered a mosaic of lovely views to enjoy.

One spring Hugh loaned out some dogs to some folks out at Chandalar Lake. These kids were too young and inexperienced to transport the dogs back to Coldfoot. It would be up to the musher to go and retrieve his beloved pooches.

Hugh set off early on a Saturday morning in late April. It was a few weeks after Easter; all he brought with him from Coldfoot to eat was a sandwich and a bag full of jelly beans for his personal 'fuel'. There were still a few feet of snow on the ground but fortunately the trail was packed down and in decent shape. He was going for a 'wilderness walkabout' with few provisions in honor of his hero John Muir. It was a lonely feeling walking those seventy miles in the springtime; he was nervous that bears would be out and about. A few hours out, Hugh noticed a bunch of moose that were huddled together; they were fighting off any potential attacks from the local wolves.

The following afternoon he finally made it to his buddy Mike Jayne's place. It was quite the adventure but seeing the looks of excitement and happiness on two of his female leaders', Shyela and Gracie's faces, brought warmth to his heart.

A few days later the pack of eight dogs lead Hugh back to the cozy confines of Coldfoot. This was quite the adventure for Hugh to undertake having just finished the Quest a month earlier with a frozen foot. Sometimes in life you just have to deal with the situation and hope for the best. A true musher will do whatever it takes to make sure their dawgs are safe and healthy.

So how does a person freeze a foot during a race? From what I remember it happened just before Slaven's Cabin on the Yukon River; one of the most remote areas of the Yukon Quest trail. It was extremely cold that morning; at fifty below things tend to freeze up rather quickly.

Photo by Jjay Levy

Hugh wasn't thinking properly, he was dehydrated and exhausted from the long run from Trout Creek Cabin and his spirits were demoralized. He had made a big mistake by not drinking enough fluids. Thinking that the best idea was to just lie down for a bit, he stretched out onto of his sled bag as all of us pooches curled up, feeling quite comfortable in our custom made dog jackets. Hours passed when suddenly a light appeared, two other mushers were heading down the trail coming towards us; it was

Thomas Tetz and John Schandelmeir. These guys are two of the race's greatest mushers ever. John had given Hugh the nickname 'Gypsy Musher' because people never knew where in Alaska he and his dogs would be living next.

Thomas yelled out, "Hugh! Is that you?"

Startled, Hugh jumped up and faced the two men. He was out of sorts. For some reason the only words that came from his lips were, "George Bush, is that you?"

The silly things that come out of humans mouths...

Feeling refreshed, we continued on our way with our two mushing friends. The funny thing about racing is that even though we compete against one another in dire situations we are obligated to help our fellow humans and their dog teams too! As the race progressed, Hugh could feel that something was not right. He had no feeling in his left foot. By the time he reached Carl Cochrane's cabin, just outside of Circle, his toes had blistered up nearly two inches. The other mushers warned him that it was dangerous to continue on. Carl took him aside, letting Hugh know that he could handle it. "I want you to borrow my Neo Boots; they're a bit larger than yours so that swelled up foot wont hurt as much." (Hugh would make sure to return them to Carl via dogsled the following year.)

The rest of that year's race was a struggle, our team fell back a few places because of his handicap but with June Mari leading the way, we finished in 8th place. The race officials and veterinarians kept a close eye on Hugh to make sure he could take care of us properly; for without dogs, there would be no dog mushing.

By the time we returned to Coldfoot after the race there was a new surprise waiting for us. The restaurant had opened up a new bar; it was to be called, *"The Frozen Foot."*

For the next few months Hugh would be in endless pain, as his blister covered foot slowly healed resembling, at times, a slab of cooked bacon.

As the years went by lessons such as these would strengthen his spirit. One must realize that to evolve they must learn from their mistakes. Instead of buying cheaper, second hand clothes to race with, he needed to invest in better trail gear; his favorite type being the fur mitts and hats created by his native friends. It wasn't just clothing, he would learn to drink more fluid and eat consistently on the trail just as we dogs must devour our meaty treats every few hours. Much of what one attains in life begins with how they care for themselves. In the North, most mushers learn to be cheap. Things are expensive up here, yet when it comes to wearing clothes at fifty below my best advice would be to invest wisely.

Over the long run Hugh has come to realize that just like the sunrise and the sunset, life has its joys and pains as well. A person can hide inside always worried about their safety however dealing with pain sooner or later will eventually become a reality. Staying positive despite these hardships is the best way to keep the team heading in the right direction. That year was a tough one for Hugh but he never gave up.

One month after freezing his foot he actually competed in his very first Kobuk 440 race, way up northwest in Alaska's Seward Peninsula.

Photo by Nicole Faille

This event begins in the village of Kotzebue. Yes, he still had a partially frozen foot; in fact all of his toe nails had fallen off the morning of the day the race began. He was bound and determined to make up for his past mistakes; he needed to prove to himself and his dawgs that he could learn from the Quest experience. It was a tough and challenging event, especially for a rookie musher in a lot of pain. Out of fifteen teams, Laughing Eyes finished in 5th place. Believe me we were all overjoyed, smiling from ear to ear.

Chapter Six:

Iditarod VS. Yukon Quest

"Here's to Joe, and it's off we go in the land of the midnight sun. They call this race the Iditarod Trail, to me it's Redington's run, in my heart it's Redington's run.."

-Hobo Jim

Photo by Jjay Levy

Photo by Sam Harrell

Hi, I'm June-Mari, the Queen of our pack. I've been the main gal in the lead for eleven thousand mile races. Marcellus is our other main lead 'alpha' dawg; he's also been my boyfriend for the last ten years. That's quite a long time in doggie years but it feels like I fell in love with him just yesterday.

Our very first big race was the 2000 Yukon Quest. We were the smallest team in Fairbanks at the starting line with only ten dogs compared to the average of fourteen. We had no idea we were even doing a one thousand mile race...

Hugh had not mentioned that we would be travelling by sled to another country; Canada! I think he might have been a bit stressed out at the time, not only being a rookie but having to put his smashed up sled back together after the infamous moose encounter. Sure, our team had done the Copper Basin 300 earlier that season as well as a few other mid-distance races, however, this time our talents would be tested to the limit.

Leaving the big city of Fairbanks, Marcellus and I led the team down the Chena River wondering where we'd be heading to that day. We could tell something special was happening, for there were thousands of race fans lining the trail to cheer us on our way. Guiding our sled was the same, silly, smiley faced boy wearing his favorite Chicago Bears hat. Hugh was full of vim and vigor as he anticipated what lay ahead—the challenge of a lifetime! He had dreamed of this day for many moons, and now it was finally time for us to set forth on this amazing journey together.

Hugh would learn along the way that traveling by dog team was enjoyable as long as he learned to care for us properly. Not only would we need good food but proper care of our feet and bodies too. Proper care included putting on nylon booties to protect our paw's pads. Special oils and creams would be used to lubricate our feet as well as to massage our worn out muscles. Feeling his hands caress my fatigued body sure did help to bring my spirits up quickly. A cozy bed of straw helped to insure a better rest also.

Photo by Bob Hallinen

Hugh would learn by watching other mushers care for their teams. Racing really wasn't just about how tough you were physically; it was about how tough you were mentally. Just a smile, or perhaps the whistling of a tune, could perk all of us up. Why would anyone feel bad when we are all so fortunate to be a part of this unique dog mushing scene? That first year traveling up the Yukon River was a heavenly experience. The sunrise over American Summit just outside of Eagle, coming into the historical city of Dawson, the mystical hills of the Klondike — these moments will be etched in our souls forevermore.

Those final few miles as we neared the finish line were magical. As a team we were in awe of all that had been accomplished. We might not have been up there with the frontrunners but we had tried to do our best and that's what mattered most. Now, some people don't understand why we put ourselves through so much; aching muscles, weary eyes, tired from little sleep. What they don't realize is that we are honoring the land around us, as well as the ways of our ancestors. For us, this isn't just a race; this is a celebration of the Northern lifestyle. Our spirits were soaring!

That first year of competing in the Quest we didn't even make the top ten, finishing 13th out of thirty-one teams.

Our team was given the coveted Challenge of the North award, which is given to the musher and dog team who have to overcome the most obstacles. From Circle City all the way to Whitehorse — some 700 miles — our team consisted of only seven pooches.

Hugh had borrowed a few dogs before the race to help fill out the squad. He would learn in the first few hundred miles that if a musher does not have a proper bond with any of their dogs the relationship will not last very long in races. Huskies need to be loved consistently, to know their mushers; or else, they might become disheartened, losing their desire to continue on.

We dawgs always knew that it wasn't about who barked the loudest at the starting line but who gave the most from their heart along the way. There are many winners in any sport no matter what place you come in. As long as we gave it our best shot we can always hold our heads high. Besides, our story was just beginning. We were new to this school and there was still a lot to learn.

As the years flew by, Laughing Eyes Kennel — slowly through experience — climbed higher in the standings of the Yukon Quest, typically finishing in the top five.

Though Hugh had fallen in love with the Quest's trail, it was the thought of competing in the Iditarod race that had captured his imagination initially. Hugh had run out of money driving from Chicago to Alaska and spent a winter doing construction work in Corvallis, Oregon.

While living there he purchased Lew Freedman's book '*Iditarod Classics*', Lew wove a tale of different mushers' experiences that was mesmerizing. Hugh was so enthralled that he immediately spent a month's wages on an airline ticket so he could fly up and experience the start of the 'Last Great Race' in Anchorage. He had no more spending money when he arrived, thus he stayed at *"Bean's Café"* — a homeless shelter — for a few nights. It was a ruff existence but hearing the roar of each dog team as they departed the starting line made up for it.

Once the ceremonial start was finished Hugh walked from Anchorage to Eagle River along the highway, finally getting picked up by a Russian fellow named Yaraslov.

"Where to?" he asked.

"I'm heading to Wasilla to see the start of the Iditarod tomorrow", was Hugh's reply. That night Hugh shivered away in subzero temps. But he wasn't suffering; the chance to see his mushing heroes—folks like Swenson, Linder and Riddles—take off the following morning was more than worth the discomfort. It was a long night though, for he would spend it trying to catch some Zz's while camped out in a port-o-potty.

Where there's a will, there's a way- no matter how penniless one might be!

In 2004 Hugh decided to take us on a new journey, we were finally heading for Nome!

The Iditarod was created by Joe Redington to help promote dog mushing in Alaska; we were excited to finally be a part of it. Fans realized that even though we were deemed rookies with five Quest competitions under our belt, our squad had a leg-up on the competition. Hugh's goal for this race was simple; we were just gonna chase his buddy, Timmy Osmar, around.

Tim is one of the best mushers there is; we realized our odds of doing well were elevated if we could hang with this champion musher for a few days... hopefully.

The modern day Iditarod is a race for wealthy people compared to the laid back Yukon Quest competition. Many of the competitors we were going up against had done this race dozens of times. Hugh realized it would be difficult to surpass any of these professional mushers, but that was no excuse to not, at least, try our hardest.

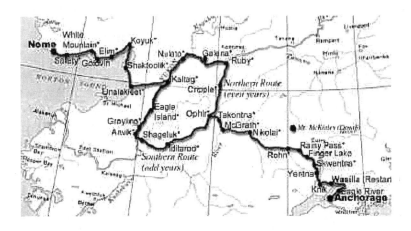

The race went surprisingly well; we finished in 22nd place out of sixty-five teams, earning the 'Rookie of the Year Award'. It was tough travelling on a trail that none of us had been on before. We learned that the western coast of Alaska has some brutal weather. Massive windstorms are created from the Ocean slamming into a land mass with few trees for protection. Numerous 'blowholes' were encountered, which teams must mush through.

Challenges such as these are what events like this are all about. That's why Hugh is constantly bringing our team to different areas of Alaska, and Canada, as well as other countries; his true love is for exploring, witnessing how others live, their unique cultures and the wondrous landscapes on other parts of the planet. There's more to life than running around on the same track all the time, after all.

People often ask which race is tougher, the Yukon Quest or the Iditarod; My reply? It depends on what type of mood Mother Nature is in. The Quest typically has colder overall temperatures as it is run one month earlier in the year. As stated earlier, Alaska's coast from Unalakleet all the way into Nome is often treacherous with massive windstorms; these ground blizzards can halt a dog team in their tracks. (That being said, in 2010 the Quest had extreme winds from start to finish)

With conditions such as these it doesn't matter how much work crews do to put in a quality trail for mushers to travel over; Mother Nature can wipe away a decent surface within minutes. A drifted in trail forces mushers and their teams to move at a snail's pace compared to their average speed. Situations such as these certainly test the will and spirits of both man and beast. In some respects it's hard to compare these races because they both have very unique character-istics to them. The Quest has Eagle Summit, which

has ruined many a team's race, while the Iditarod offers obstacles such as The Happy River Steps and Dalzell Gorge.

Photo by Loren Holmes

Each race has numer-ous volunteers, though the Quest seems to have more responsibility placed upon fewer people's shoulders. The Iditarod, being a bit older, is looked upon as being the larger of the two events — though internationally the internet is providing a larger audience for both events on a yearly basis.

Back in the early 70's, when Joe Redington's Iditarod was unfolding, the technology they used to provide food and care to the dogs was not very advanced. In fact, there was only one veterinarian for the *whole* race. Nowadays, scores of veterinarians fly up the first weekend of March every year to volunteer, and be on Dr. Stu Nelson's vet staff.

Scientists from universities across the country study teams on a yearly basis seeking to discover how these animals come to be some of the healthiest critters on this planet. Travelling further than any other animal, numerous husky dogs are capable of running over a hundred miles, daily, for weeks at a time.

Annie and her daughter Jewel leading the way.

On the Quest side, Dr. Kathleen McGill and her crew have improved conditions for all of the dogs too. Not only have feeding regimens improved, but ointments—used to care for their bodies through massage—come in various styles for the pooches to enjoy. Foot salves are a must in order to ensure healthy pads and paws. Vitamin supplements are also administered as well as antacids to help stop any ulcer issues which periodically come about due to the difficult daily stresses that are a part of 'trail life'.

Dog jackets and harness designs have been altered throughout the years in order to place less stress on dogs' bodies, comfort them while sleeping as well protect pooches from weather extremes; the cold, the wind, or the sun.

Many folks believe that faster, lighter, high tech sleds are responsible for quicker race times. There is truth to this but the quality of dog care, animal husbandry, and evolution of race technique is a major component in the overall performance of the average field. Having deep pockets is a big advantage for those obsessed with winning, but for the everyday musher, high tech food, clothing and sleds has made our journeys smoother and—hopefully—safer in the long run.

Photo by Nicole Faille

From an 'old school' sled dog's perspective I would have to say that the Quest is a throw back race to a bygone era where 'gold fever' hung over the land. Whether it is traveling along the Yukon River near the gold fields of Dawson, or winding one's way down Birch Creek heading toward Circle City, there is a presence in the air, a mystical feeling. You are in awe at what the eyes have seen, spellbound, for nothing in the *world* compares. The stories that have been written by Jack London, Robert Service, and others, pay homage to a time when acquiring gold and riches was the adventure to be had. Only the wise among us realize that the true gold lay in the land, the beauty around them. Folks back then were using dog teams for more important things than just racing; they needed their furry friends helping them in order to survive. They might be missionaries, miners, Natives or mail drivers; without dog power, life would be much more difficult in the severe wintertime season.

Individual dogs were as expensive as five hundred dollars each; an amount of money that still buys a descent husky over a hundred years later. The coveted job to have at the time was that of a mail carrier. The only problem was, even at sixty below, if you didn't finish your job on time there were dozens of others waiting to take it away after you were relieved of your duties.

In parts of the North there are stories told of haunted hotels and houses, but when approaching the Dawson region of the Yukon I realized that this whole area had a 'unique aura' around it. Though the world might be in the 21st century now, there will always be a part a Dawson's psyche that will forever remain stuck in the late 1800's.

Dawson City, Yukon

When out on the Quest trail, with fewer mushers in the field on an annual basis, you spend a lot
more time alone just with your dawgs, the land and
your inner thoughts. It's a time to appreciate the land
and the amazing freedoms we have here in the far
North. This race challenges you with its long stretches
between checkpoints, some of them being over two
hundred miles apart. Training your team not only to
be in great physical shape but to be mentally tough
ensures success on these longer stretches. The musher
and dawgs must be of one spirit, obstacles are certain
to appear eventually along the way which must be
overcome. Patience when handling these different
situations is paramount for tiny mistakes may lead to
larger troubles; we all know how small problems can
snowball. During these longer stretches a musher
must keep a keen eye on the dawgs, watching their
gaits, as well as making sure their appetites stay
healthy. If a musher notices a dawg that does not look
right one must immediately stop the team to see what

89

the issue is. Maybe the dog is stressed from being up front and would prefer to be farther back in the team for awhile. Perhaps it's just a neckline that is on the backside of their leg? There are numerous predicaments to deal with, letting the situation linger will only make things worse. If a dog is obviously worn out, take them and put them in the sled to be carried for a ways; it's amazing what a wee bit of rest will do, especially in the heat of the day. A sore wrist may be mended just through some simple massage. On warmer days dawgs may be rotated and given brief breaks in the sled just to save their energy for later on down the trail. What is good for one dawg will always benefit the wellness of the team in the long run.

Known as the "Indy 500" of dog racing, seeking to compare the Iditarod with the Quest is akin to the difference between New York City and Dawson City. It just has more of everything except for the most important one, the number of miles. While some mushers prefer the smaller race venues the Iditarod has a massive following compared to any other dog mushing race in the world. On a yearly basis twice as many mushers sign up for this race, usually around sixty-five to eighty folks from around the world come for fun; the chance to enjoy and finish Redington's run.

In any sporting event there are lots of egos competing against one another, that's no exception here. Not all of the mushers exactly see eye to eye, yet their love for this race in undiminished. They all live for a chance to run the race with their dawgs, cautiously gambling with numerous moves throughout the grueling nine or ten day race to win their share of the prize. In this day and age there are dozens of outstanding teams competing on a yearly basis. What sets apart the contenders from the pretenders is experience, innovation, a desire to strive for personal excellence. As the decades have passed finishing times have dramatically gotten faster. What once took up to a month to complete now takes just over a week. Many mushers watch each other, always seeking to learn and gain a competitive edge. The people *not* to worry about are typically those who seem to think they know it all. A true champion never stops wanting to learn.

Photo by Nicole Faille

Through the process of learning more about their dawgs and the land they improve themselves as well.

I LOVE both of these races immensely, not for the competition, but for what they stand for—FREEDOM. Perhaps one of these years someone will create the 'Master Race', from Whitehorse to Nome, Idit-aQuest, anyone? Hopefully we all can agree by now that both of these events are treasures for the entire world to celebrate.

Photo by john Wagner/Associated Press

Having done both races consecutively for eight years in a row we have come to the conclusion that what matters most is that the dog team enjoys each event tremendously. We have proven that participating in one event creates a better dog team for further competitions. The pooches' bodies become 'hardened in'; their heads are attuned to what's expected of them and their hearts are ready to soar!

Most mushers, as well as their dogs, could use the added experience too; that's why I'm always mystified that many famous Iditarod mushers have yet to do the Quest. If they only knew how much of life they were missing out on! The energy of hundreds of beasts flying down the trail in search of their next conquest is just awesome; that's why these events have such a large worldwide following. It isn't only about who wins but the sense of adventure, of people seeking to conquer difficult obstacles, to feel truly *ALIVE.*

Photo by Carol Falsetta

Much like any other venue, there are quite a bit of negative politics involved in the mushing scene. Unfortunately, that's just a part of being human these days I guess. Hopefully in the future more mushers will learn to respect each other despite any differences they might have, so many ugly rumors are created on a yearly basis just to bring the competition down a notch. Everyone wants to be the 'king of the hill', to be noticed more, etc. The weakest musher is the human who wants to be the greatest dog musher on the planet. You know why? Because any

true musher just wants to have the greatest dog team on the planet. *Comprende?* This isn't a 'me' sport it's a 'we' sport. For the sake of our future, it is important to be kind to your neighbors on the trail. We all know at the finish line—whether it be in Nome, Whitehorse or points in between—it's the look of LOVE shining throughout each dawg's exquisite eyes as they stare at you which determines whether or not you are a true Dog-Man. Hopefully then, you will be the winner of the greatest race imaginable.

Photo by Tamra Reynolds

Chapter Seven:
Kotzebue and Alaska's other Jewels

"I think over again and again my small adventures, my fears, those small ones that seemed so big, those vital things I had to get and reach, yet there is only one great thing: to live and see the great day that dawns, and the light that fills the world."

-Eskimo proverb

Photo by Nicole Faille

How ya doing? My name is Uncus. I'm not the pretty dawg up in lead in the team; I'm the fella right in front of the sled doing all of the muscle work. It can get a little dangerous back there —especially on tight twisty trails when I have to jump across the gang line to avoid running into stuff. I guess you could say I'm kind of like a linebacker in football; not the biggest or fastest dog, but pound for pound nobody is as strong as me. I've raced in eight 1,000 mile races in the wheel position. The Gypsy Musher named me after a character in a book called, *"Last of the Mohicans"* by James Fenimore Cooper. I guess I'm just one of a kind.

Out of all the places in Alaska and the Yukon that I've seen, my favorites to visit are the unique native villages spread throughout the North. When we first started traveling around Alaska it was the Athabascan people we visited the most. Going to places like Nenana, Minto, Tanana or Tok is always enjoyable. It is fun visiting with extended family as us 'Yukon River Dawgs' are known. When we started racing in the Quest we traveled through country inhabited by the Han, Northern Tutchone as well as the Southern Tutchone, and Tagish Peoples.

On the Iditarod route the country in which we started off was primarily white folk, though the land will always be that of the Tanana. A few hundred miles into the race we would enter the Upper

Kuskokwim, from there was the land of the Koukon. Heading west reaching Alaska's coast we were now in the land of the Inupiaq Eskimo's of Norton Sound, the Kotzebue area. Each January we would travel to Bethel to participate in the Kuskokwim 300 mile sled dog race. Down there the folks are central Yupik.

Photo by Nicole Faille

It can be a little bit nerve racking flying around on planes before and after races, sometimes via Alaska Airlines, but once we've landed that's when the real fun begins. Exploring new sights, sounds and smells is what being a dawg is all about! I feel sorry for other dawgs who are not lucky enough to experience the pleasure of traveling through Alaska's village communities for they are the true Heart of The Greatland. Every year a few weeks after the Iditarod has finished, and we've rested up a bit. Our team will load up into a plane and fly a few hours northwest to the Eskimo community of Kotzebue.

This far North in the Arctic the weather is a daily challenge with constant winds coming from the ocean. The Beauty of this region is breathtaking too, vast valleys stretching for dozens of miles in every direction. This area, in some history books, is known as the land bridge between North America and Asia, though many locals prefer to call it an 'ice bridge'.

The first week of April is the Kobuk 440 which goes from Kotzebue through several Eskimo villages heading straight east. Having reached the village of Kobuk, teams loop around, seeking to return to where they started out from. It's a fun race—unlike other events, all the teams start out at the same time; this is called a mass start. Once the signal gun is shot off, mayhem ensues. Imagine fifteen to twenty pumped up twelve-dog teams flying out of the chute all at the same time. My tail wags just thinking about it!

For the Gypsy Musher, we as dawgs realized that this was the best place for him to learn how to become a better dog musher. Many of Alaska's most talented dog musher's live and train in this area, John Baker, the Nelsons, Schaeffers, and Iten family, just to name a few.

Anytime we race here we're hoping to beat folks such as these. We are smart enough to realize that even if we might not get that championship trophy, having the opportunity to learn from more experienced people is a good thing. People sharing knowledge is best for all in the long run. Happy dawgs means happy trails.

I've seem some beautiful sights up on Alaska's Northwest Coast, one that will always stand out in my memory happened in the early morning hours as we were traveling from Selawik on our way back to

Kotzebue. As we marched across the ocean's frozen ice a mist rose creating a fog in which we could barely see a few hundred yards in front of our master's headlamp. Yet above us the stars were out and florescent green auroras snaked their way across the sky. As I glanced to the left of the team I noticed a lovely full moon, the rising mist gave the moon a purplish hue. It was a wondrous sight to behold. I sure was happy once we got back on land again. For you see, out there on the ocean all there is to see for miles is the color of white, there are no trees in these parts, barely a bush or two.

Photo by Nicole Faille

It's interesting to watch how the local Native Alaskans relate to their dawgs. They give them respect but treat them as the animals they are and not just house pets. Natives are a very efficient people, it's cool to watch how John Baker has trained his dawgs to lay on their backs as he puts their booties on them. Having traveled so much throughout my fifteen years here in Alaska it's easy to tell which mushers and dawgs respect each other, knowing one another's thoughts and moods almost as if they were one spirit. In a real dog team the dawgs and the musher are of one mind. Racing is fun but the shared journey together is really what it's all about. If you're not enjoying life then sometimes it's better to find a different trail to travel upon.

Photo by Nicole Faille

The other major mid-distance race we participate in each year takes place in the village of Bethel. The Kuskokwim 300 runs to Aniak and back. Through relatively flat terrain compared to what we see in the Quest, the K300 can be quite the workout. All the top Iditarod mushers show up to this event-King, Buser, Mitch Seavey, Lance Mackey, Aaron Burmeister, Ray Redington, and the Smyth Brothers. We like visiting Bethel because host families such as Pat Barrett or the Klem family even let us sleep in their homes. They are great friends to our kennel. Each time we visit they'll even cook up ribs and all sorts of meaty-treaties for us. Around these parts a dawg will need a lot of extra weight. The wind gusts here can sap our energy real fast when the weather gets sketchy out.

The strangest year we ever had on the Kusko 300 was when the temperatures were actually a bit *too* warm. A few days before the race was to begin...it was *raining*. Once we set off from the starting line, we could tell that it would be more like a survival course than a speedway. A few dozen miles out of town the splashing began, for over seventy miles of river there was open water known as overflow. At times it was a few feet deep which was a little wet for my taste. This was a pretty demanding environment, especially when we could see that all of the trail markers were floating down the river. Hmmm...which way should we go? That year, just a few miles from the finish line, we had to camp out in a local village because conditions were just too dangerous.

Ambler, Alaska   *Photo by Nicole Faille*

Sometimes in life there are things that are more important than what place you finish or how much money you make. When dealing with Mother Nature safety must always come first.

The beauty of dog mushing, and places like Bethel or Kotzebue, is found in the local native's culture, how they honor their land and ancestors. There's a spirit here that resonates throughout the people. It's why we love Alaska so, and can't wait to come back to these parts and visit again soon.

Chapter Eight:

2012 Yukon Quest- It Took a While, but we did it in Style

"Is everybody in? The ceremony is about to begin. Let me tell you about heartache... wandering, wandering in a hopeless night. Out here in the perimeter there are no stars, out here we is stone, immaculate. Riders on the storm..."

-J.D. Morrison

Photo by Sweetpea Marie

Photo by Nicole Faille

So, you would like to know how I came to be the famous *Walter*?

Well, I'm tall and brown and quite furry; sixty-five pounds of brute force with a heart to match. Some folks say I was named after a football player, Walter Payton, from the Chicago Bears. He is Hugh's favorite football player of all time.

It wasn't because of all the awards he won, including the Super Bowl but the way "Sweetness", number thirty-four, approached life. He had the heart of a lion, and people could see it in the way he played the game. There were many years when Walter's team was not very competitive yet he still gave every ounce of his energy doing his best in every game. Walter Payton had that positive energy that just makes people smile.

My other friends tell me that I was named after an Indian, an Athabascan fiddler by the name of Walter Newman. Wherever Mr. Newman went he made friends because of his exuberant personality. Folks still speak about him with smiles on their faces to this day. I'd like to think that I was named after both of these people. Most folks are named after people whose spirits have influenced their lives. Often times out on the trail I can feel both Walters' spirits within my very soul.

Now some of you may have heard of my favorite sister, Annie; not only is she one of the most hyper ladies I know, she's just as talented too. Along with our brother Watson, We grew up together and moved up the ranks of our kennel's dog team. Having done eight one thousand mile races by now, the experiences we learned from along the way taught us how to move up to the front of our pack.

In dog mushing there are all sorts of leaders. There are 'Gee-Haw leaders' who are good at following directions or 'speed leaders' who are up in front when running across flat surfaces such as rivers. 'Mountain dogs' are like big locomotive engines when put in front of the team going up steep, twisty trails-they'll get you over that mountain pass through the fiercest blizzards. I'd like to think I am a bit of each kind of leader, a renaissance dog. I might not be as fast as some of the younger kids I am competing against these days, but often the slow and steady teams who are consistent win in the long run. Knowing how to conserve one's energy creates a stronger you.

For this year's Quest Annie would not even be participating, yet many of her offspring would be my teammates. Sharing the duties in the lead position, besides myself were my nieces, Juanita and Jewel, their brother George, as

Photo by Vince Federoff

well as the lovely Delilah. Most of us, having done the Quest before, realized that we were once again on the adventure of a lifetime.

Not as well known as the famous Iditarod race, the Quest has its own unique natural treasures to enjoy; an immense landscape with unparalleled history and numerous obstacles to encounter. The daunting Eagle Summit as well as various levels of overflow water to deal with at fifty below. On some longer stretches of the Yukon River, it can be hard just to find where the trail is, yet with a will there is a way. Having participated in this race half a dozen times it is always nice to have experience on your side. Unfortunately in the 2011 Yukon Quest, our team endured one of the most horrific experiences after enjoying one of the greatest runs in Yukon Quest history.

Photo by S.G. Sea

For over a week we lead the race, never seeing another team on the trail; setting a pace that no other squad could match. At point we were ahead of all the other teams by half a day. Our trouble began as we came to the end of Birch Creek about fifteen miles from the checkpoint of Central. We passed by two snowmachiner's who warned us of some dangerous trail that was up ahead around the river's bend. There was overflow water a few football fields in length with an ice crust barely a centimeter's width. As we approached this dangerous area our dog musher, Hugh, would take over the lead command, going in front of the team and walking us through water that was up to his knee caps. What made the situation far worse was the fact that the temperatures were already at fifty below zero. Just to get across this stretch

Photos by Tracie Stalker

of water took nearly an hour's time. All the dogs would have to have their booties replaced, it was easier for some of us furrier canines as we were smart enough to rub our backs in the snow and shake off some of the cold water before we continued on. Our

musher on the other hand was in quite a predicament as his suit and parka were now crusted in ice. His boots were filled with water as the cold temps slowly solidified them, compressing his feet inside. We could sense his anguish as he begged for mercy, praying that he would not lose any of his body parts to the unforgiving arctic conditions. We were worried. After all, it was fifty below zero at the time. Sadly for myself, my tail suffered the worst out of all us dawgs.

The rest of the team had to carry me in the sled into Central which was still a few hours away. Arriving in the checkpoint the veterinarians discovered that I would be better off left behind here so the vets could care for my frozen, injured tail. It was so cold that the only way for Hugh to get his clothes off was to climb into a hot shower to thaw out his frozen boots. Fortunately for him, none of his body parts were frozen, unlike the 2005 race when he almost lost his left foot. It was tough not being able to be a part of the team for the rest of the race; however, sometimes in life situations like these arise. Knowing that the worst part of the trail still lay ahead, all I could do was wish them luck. The next morning I could tell that something was wrong; all of the people following the race were worried. Hugh and his team had been stuck on the notorious Eagle Summit as a ferocious windstorm slammed into them. While trying to ascend the Summit one of our dogs Geronimo, regurgitated, and then aspirated (inhaled) some food while running, filling up his lungs. Hugh tried to give him mouth to nose CPR to no avail.

Photo by Tracie Stalker

A rescue team would eventually be

sent out to take the squad to the next checkpoint, Mile 101. It's a moment none of us will ever get over, losing a fellow mushing warrior whether it is during a storm or because of old age is always heart wrenching. That's why we must always treasure our family and the honest friendships that we are so fortunate to have.

Photo by Tracie Stalker

Our team's goal for the 2012 Quest race was to honor Geronimo's spirit by giving it our all. We wanted to win, not necessarily by what place we finished, but by how we performed on a daily basis. Having done this race several times already I was excited to be out and about playing with dozens of other dog teams as we travelled from Fairbanks going towards Whitehorse. It's always nice heading in this direction, as the trail always seems to be a bit safer winding its way south instead of going north in the wintertime.

What set this year's race apart from previous ones were the temperatures; they ranged from the mid-twenties, all the way up to above freezing. Humans down south might think that we would enjoy these warmer temperatures but they are actually far more difficult to travel in for us furry beasts of the north. The trail will be much softer; creating a punchy snow that often times resembles quicksand as we slowly chug through it.

Hugh was smart enough to bring along lots of fish to snack us, as water is a key element for keeping us hydrated, and fish contains a lot of water. A few hundred miles down the trail we reached the hallowed ground where all of our misfortunes occurred the previous year; the notorious Eagle Summit.

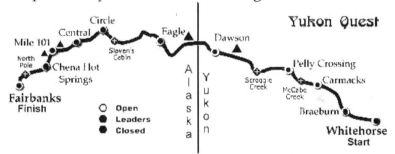

Anchoring down the sled next to a tripod on the mountain, Hugh reached into his sled bag and pulled out a picture of our beloved buddy Geronimo. He pinned it on to the marker and said a prayer for this beautiful animal's spirit. This spot will always have a special meaning to us, we all know in the back of our minds that Geronimo is a part of our team and always will be.

For most of the race our team took turns sharing the lead with the rest of the front runners; Brent Sass, Lance Mackey and Allen Moore.

By the time we reached Dawson City we were in 3ʳᵈ place, just a few hours behind Mr. Moore's fine squad.

Photo by Tracie Stalker

A thirty-six hour mandatory layover is required in Dawson City each year; it gives us dogs and our musher a chance to relax and rest up for the second half of the journey. This is where we try to gain some weight back as well as heal any potential soreness the dogs or musher might have. Even though we were in 3ʳᵈ place at this point in the race, Hugh was quite worried. There were a few dogs with foot issues that needed to be cared for through the use of creams and ointments. His biggest problem was our appetites; the toughest as-

Photo by Pat Kane

pect concerning warm temperatures is that it causes many pooches to become finicky eaters. Hugh would have to find a way to get some food into our stomachs. He might not be the smartest of mushers yet he's wise enough to learn through past experiences wheth-

114

er they be good or bad. Hugh went over to the local grocery store and bought some tasty human foods that he knew would be irresistible for us dawgs to chow down. Drum sticks, turkey, you name it, added to dog kibble these fatty meats helped to revive our appetites.

Two veterinarians from Norway, Per and Hannah, were assigned to look over our team. They gave Hugh advice on which of us needed care and other information that was priceless in aiding our successful trip to Whitehorse. Once our required layover was finished, harnesses and booties were once again fastened on as we set off towards the next check point — Pelly Crossing.

Allen Moore and Lance Mackey's teams were quite a ways ahead but our team was not about to start stressing. Patience is always an ally in dog mushing.

A few hours outside of Scroggie Creek, we passed by the two other dog teams who were bedded down in a windstorm up in the Black Hills. We were the first team to reach Scroggie but we all knew that this race was far from over. Each musher was jockeying for position as our three elite squads separated from the rest of the field.

Photo by Tracie Stalker

Hugh had some bad news to tell the race officials when we arrived. There had been a miscommunication in Dawson. Unfortunately his axe, which is mandatory gear, had been left behind. Hugh realized we would be penalized for this but he also knew that in life it is wise to admit one's mistakes. Small problems have a way of growing larger when they are ignored. Our team received the mandatory thirty minute penalty for this miscue of not having all of the required gear with us. Who knew if this penalty would affect the outcome of the race? I'll tell you what though; the dogs really didn't mind getting the extra half-an-hour of rest. Sometimes difficulties can be blessings; it's all a matter of one's perspective. Learning to stay positive in difficult situations is always an advantage!

Having completed our rest break we continued on down the trail in pursuit of the two other teams that had passed us while we were sleeping. Later that afternoon we camped out with Lance and Allen's dog teams as we all waited for the sun's warmth to lose some of its intensity. The warm weather was playing havoc with our digestive systems; most of the dogs on our squad were having major gas issues.

Photo by Tracie Stalker

Some people might be surprised to know that mushers often help each other out on the trail. Lance Mackey bartered with Hugh, trading some diarrhea medication in exchange for some dog booties. Hugh let Allen Moore borrow an extra Leatherman tool for the rest of the race. In life it is always smart to help those in need, especially in the

116

harsh environment of the Arctic—you never know when it might be your turn to seek some help.

The last few days of the race it was obvious that Mr. Moore's team as well as ours would be vying for the championship. Our squads exchanged the lead back and forth, rarely being more than ten minutes apart from one another. Coming into the final checkpoint of Braeburn, we found out that Allen's lead had grown; his team was now fifteen minutes ahead of us. At this point in the race the extra half hour penalty was served. Hugh seemed a bit despondent, feeling as if he had let down his team as well as the fans rooting for us.

We all watched as Allen's team left Braeburn nearly an hour before we were allowed to head for home, the finish line! There was now less than a hundred miles left in the race; an hour's lead was nearly insurmountable to overtake. By now we were all praying for a miracle, the gathering crowd waited in anticipation of our departure, Hugh was wise enough to face his back towards all of the humans avoiding any distractions. He concentrated on making sure our booties were on nice and tight, our harnesses were on correctly, and most importantly, that we were all focused on doing our best. He lovingly reassured all of

us about how special we are to him, what an incredible journey we had been on.

Belly scratches and light massages woke us from our

Photo by Tracie Stalker

deep sleep, as well as some tasty broth to nourish our thirst.

"You ready Walter? Let's do this."

Photo by Tracie Stalker

Late that afternoon our time had finally arrived to see what we had within our hearts. I had the honor of leading us for the last leg of the race. To be honest I was a bit reluctant to have all that pressure set on my shoulders, but once we were out of the checkpoint it was time to 'Rock and Roll'.

Braeburn is one of Hugh's favorite spots along the trail; his buddy, Steve, runs the restaurant there with some of the best food in the Yukon Territory. We had been over this section of trail to Whitehorse many times, this was our backyard! It was time to play; we were off in search of our elusive prey.

Photo by Susan Smalley Stevenson

Heading south on the Dawson trail we realized that if there was any chance of winning many minutes would have to be made up in the hills before we reached the last section of trail that follows the Takhini and Yukon Rivers into the finish line. The temperatures were still quite warm—in the high 20's —but fortunately that night there was a wild wind storm that felt like air conditioning. For the first fifty miles I was teamed up with Juanita in lead; we set off at an all out lope in pursuit of Mr. Moore's squad.

Photo by Tracie Stalker

Every hill Hugh would jump off the sled and start running as he encouraged us on, praising our valiant effort, "Good dogs, good dogs!" Just before reaching the Takhini River we were told by a crossing guard that the other team was now only fifteen minutes ahead of us. In that first fifty mile stretch we had already shaved a half-hour off their lead.

We kept following the trail down to the river when Hugh suddenly stopped the team. He quickly reached into the sled bag and gave us our last snack of soaked dog kibble. This energy boost enabled us to kick it into gear for the final few dozen miles.

The competition in long-distance mushing is so intense that every second on the trail counts. The more efficient mushers, and dog teams, are not only gifted runners, but have healthy appetites too!

Once we reached the river Hugh shut his head-lamp off, we were now in "stealth mode" and the hunt was on.

As we crept closer to the other team their scent on the trail became more intense in my nostrils. Ten miles further down the trail we glanced ahead and re-ceived an amazing adrenaline rush! Just around the bend a musher's headlamp appeared bobbing back and forth. It was Allen Moore's squad; at that mo-ment, we knew the race was on!

The strangest sight I saw during this race oc-curred a few moments later, rounding the river's bend all of our doggie ears stood at attention—"What was that?"

Were we all dreaming, or are those human voices whispering? Just off to the side of the trail were thirty spectators watching the front-runners come through. Not one of these humans had their head-lamps on and neither did Hugh. A voice rang out say-ing, "Go get 'em Hughie!" It was legendary Yukon Quest musher, Frank Turner. Hugh replied giving thanks to everyone for keeping their headlamps off so that the dogs would not be startled.

As we continued on we could hear people en-couraging us, "Go Get Em!" A few miles later we were now less than a half-a-mile behind 1st place, and for some inexplicable reason Hugh decided to turn his headlamp back on. I suppose he thought it was the gentlemanly thing to do; though in racing terms, it was a big mistake. Allen suddenly turned around, realizing that it was going to be a battle to the finish.

Though we were moving fast at this time, for some reason my legs couldn't reach a higher gear. After all we had run over nine hundred and eighty miles by this point; I was starting to feel my age I guess.

Quickly stopping the team, Hugh was forced to switch me out with an aspiring younger leader named George who also happens to be Juanita's brother.

The other team pulled even further ahead while we were stopped. However switching out the lead dogs increased our speed dramatically, as we quickly narrowed the distance within the next twenty minutes.

With the two faster, younger inexperienced siblings up in front we were now just a few feet behind the other team. Passing underneath the Takhini Bridge there was now just over ten miles to the finish in downtown Whitehorse. We were hot on the other team's heels when our next obstacle occurred. One of our newest dogs Gringo, who is a year older than me, could not keep the pace and was starting to slow down our momentum. Again Hugh stopped the team, quickly placing Gringo into the sled bag.

Believe it or not, sometimes when a musher takes a dog from the team and puts them in the sled the overall team speed actually gets faster. After all, a dog team can only go as fast as its slowest dog.

Gringo now safely secured in the sled, we resumed chasing after our prey once again. With five miles left we finally were able to get by Mr. Moore's team. Dog mushers use ski-poles to help the dogs by pushing the sled along, but it is a rule that they must stop using them in order for a passing squad to get by. Allen was kind enough to do so. It's hard to describe the electricity of a moment such as this. In the history of dog mushing few, if any, races of this length have had such a dramatic completion.

Photo by Christiane Ødegaard

We were finally in the lead now, but Allen and his team were true competitors; they had not given up hopes of winning this race. The few remaining miles both squads would be separated by *seconds*.

The beauty of this moment was that it was dog mushing at its finest, a tribute to the history of northern travelers. Two great teams with competent mushers doing their best to bring home 'the glory'; for the last half hour or so, all we dogs could hear on the trail were our mushing partners whooping and hollering up a storm, continuously cheering us on.

This was a pep-rally like no other, all of us dogs knew this was a war of determination—this was our time and no obstacle would get in our way ; this was for GERONIMO. For the last week, we had come nearly 1,000 miles all the way from Fairbanks, Alaska; our bodies might be a bit sore but our spirits were soaring! Somebody better go wake up the 'fat lady', it was almost time for her to start singing.

Less than a mile was left in the race, our epic journey was nearly complete, when glancing up ahead we all noticed a patch of ice with overflow water on the trail in front of us. Husky dogs can be quite cautious when dealing with situations like this especially after last year's ordeal. Unfortunately the young leaders up in front Juanita and George veered away from the dangerous spot and ascended up the river's bank away from the trail. Hugh stopped the sled immediately. We could tell he was distraught knowing that the other team was hot on our tails; more than likely they would pass by us at any moment. Walking up to the leaders Hugh grabbed their leader-line in order to swing the team back down onto the trail. Glancing up he realized that Mr. Moore's leaders had followed our squad and were now parallel with our team.

"Is this crazy or what?" was all Hugh could think of to say.

Without hesitation he took over the lead dawg  position, leading our team through the dangerous section of overflow water, back to safer ground. The lights of Whitehorse were

Photo by Mark Gillette

123

now in our sights, "Ain't no stopping us now, we're on the loose!"

It wasn't until the final minute or so as we meandered our way through Shipyards Park that we actually had faith in finally winning our first Yukon Quest championship.

Just before reaching the crowd at the finish line, Hugh screamed out, "Geronimo!" realizing that his spirit had been guiding us the whole way. He raised his arms to the heavens thanking not only all of us dogs in the team but every dog that has allowed him the chance to be a part of this incredible journey- we are all one spirit.

In the wee morning hours we strolled across the finish line winning the

Walter Newman   Photo by John Gaedeke

Yukon Quest by the closest time ever; just twenty-six seconds. Sure we were tired but it was time to celebrate! Steaks anyone? Hugh came up and fittingly gave me a bear hug. Walter Payton would have loved this, so would my other namesake Mr. Walter Newman.

Often in life it's not just about winning but most importantly just doing your best no matter what the outcome.

Being a true sportsman, Hugh made sure to take time to walk over and congratulate Allen Moore on having such an outstanding team as well. Allen has won several other races and realized that this one will be remembered over the ages. His impressive team would win the following year.

It sure did feel good to get all that attention and loving from so many wonderful people though to be quite honest all of us dawgs at Laughing Eyes Kennel are accustomed to being treated this way. At our kennel being treated special is how we are cared for each and every day!

And any dawg will tell you *that* is what being a true 'winning musher' is all about.

Trophy by Halin De Repivigny

Chapter Nine:

Spreading the Word

"The more that you read, the more things you will know. The more that you learn the more places you'll go."

-Dr. Seuss

Photo by Nicole Faille

Photo by Susan Smalley Stevenson

Hi, my name is Amigo! Now you might not find me in dog mushing magazines or videos but every kennel has its team players that help support the cause in one way or another. Each May the Gypsy Musher travels to the Lower 48 on his school tour, talking to kids throughout the land about the beauties of us dawgs and our northern environment.

Hugh has been traveling around the states for a few decades now, speaking in dozens of communities on a yearly basis. He's been in big cities like Chicago, New York, or Austin; it seems to me though that his favorite spots to explore are the smaller rural communities. Places such as Abingdon, Virginia, Chillicothe, Illinois, or Cannelton, Indiana, as well as numerous others. Seeing the joy in the audience member's faces as they live vicariously through our adventures is quite a heartwarming experience.

Photo by Nicole Faille

Typically, he likes to bring lots of trail gear, posters, and maps. Helping to educate Southern folk about Alaska's dog mushing lifestyle, as well as adventures we have been a part of. In places like Tennessee or Texas many of these kids have never even seen snow before. Can you imagine that? Poor things…Folks love to learn about the Iditarod, Yukon Quest and other races. What they love the most of course are the lovely and mesmerizing Dawgs.

Photo by Carrie Beeman

They learn how we are cared for: how to put booties on our feet, how harnesses and dog jackets are used and, most importantly, how to massage a dawg properly; makes me tingle inside at the thought of some warm human hands caressing my shoulders.

School kids are quite knowledgeable about dog mushing. That's because some of the most enthusiastic fans are their teachers; not only do they enjoy following the sport but teachers realize it's a great way for their students to learn! Humans and dawgs are a lot more alike than most folks realize, don't ya think?

Southern folk also realize that there is a big difference between their four legged house guests and us beasts of the North. Civilized pets are fortunate enough to go for a walk around the block, up in the Greatland a walk around the block is at least a ten to twenty mile jaunt around our neighborhood — if not more!

Huskies were meant to live in the wild where there is less traffic and more places to roam. Our energy is often limitless, if you want to really punish us all you have to do is leave us at home. A happy dawg has a healthy appetite not only for food but to get outdoors and play.

Books are what created Hugh's dream. Reading James Michener's *"Alaska"* as well as all of John Muir's novels, or native stories written by John Neirhardt, or Velma Wallis, stirred the Gypsy Musher's imagination to seek his dreams.

Photo by Robert Forto

One of Hugh's nicknames is "The Cat in the Hat." A few years ago his friend, Barb Angaiak, invited him to help promote literacy throughout Alaska. She was the President of the National Education Association of Alaska; her organization helps support teachers throughout The Greatland. Having the chance to show others the power of knowledge through reading is Hugh's mission. In fact during the Iditarod ceremonial start last year, The Cat in the Hat rode in Hugh's sled as his guest of honor. Yeah, I know it's a Cat... but we'll let that slide. After all they tend to weigh a little less in the sled than a dog would.

Photo by Scott Chesney

Laughing Eyes kennel has not won many races compared with the more experienced teams in this sport. That is why we participate so much; we are constantly trying to learn more. Life can be embarrassing at times, there will always be someone waiting to poke at or make fun of you. Yet with real friends, when times are tough, your bond will never disappear. Success is not achieved in a year, but over time. How you approach each and every day will decide whether a person is able to make it to the finish line in style. I just hope that kids of all ages see what we've gone though and adapt what they have learned to their own dreams. They might not be lucky enough to be dawgs, but humans are pretty tough critters too. You just have to realize that a lot of who you are depends not only on where you came from but the friends you surround yourself with—choose wisely my friend! Always remember that without knowing who you truly are, you can never be a good team player. Whether one wants to be a great dog musher, fireman, or business person, it is vital to realize how to take command of who you are within your heart and soul.

These days everyone has lots of energy! It comes from various sources: all of the sugar in foods, the internet as well as what we see on the television. It's difficult to have a steady pace living in this world during these chaotic times. A smart dawg learns that there are benefits to slowing down, mellowing out, and learning to listen. How will a person ever learn if they are barking at others all the time? Realize that by doing good things in life others will treat you kindly in return. The trail is never easy; challenges will always be waiting around the next bend of the river. Mother Nature's winds can be fierce at times; it's up to you to be patient, to learn that your success depends on how you approach life's daily challenges. Sure, things can get dangerous at times, yet with a will there is a way to create a more beautiful day!

Photo by Jjay Levy

Chapter Ten:
Never Stop Exploring Alaska and Beyond

"The English have loudly and openly told the world that skis and dogs are unusable in these regions and that fur clothes are rubbish. We shall see...we shall see."

-Roald Amundsen

Photo by Christiane Ødegaard

Photo by Barb Redington

Tok, Alaska...

"Why would you wanna live out there? There are no other 'top dog' mushers, hardly any trails, and not enough shopping!" Yes, I was asked this question numerous times and, YES! That is exactly why I chose to live here! Moving to Alaska, it was never my intention to keep up with the 'Joneses' of the mushing world.

Having lived in numerous regions of Alaska's Greatland and the Yukon, we have always sought peacefulness and tranquility. Avoiding stress is always high on the list here at Laughing Eyes Kennel. Now Tok might not have as many places to get groceries as the more crowded areas of the North but it has what one needs to be self sufficient without having to endure hours of traffic on a weekly basis.

Sure, there's summertime tourists who roll through town on their motorcycles or in motor homes, but they typically stay for only a day or two.

Yes, untold amounts of hunters come here in the fall to go hunting on the Taylor Highway as the Porcupine Caribou herd migrates through. Yet, only a few thousand folks live in these parts year round, many of them being our Native Athabascan neighbors. Numerous villages surround our area — Tanacross, Tetlin Junction, Mentasta, as well as Dot Lake. Having the opportunity to learn from Alaska's PEOPLE is a privilege and an honor.

As for dog mushers—there are plenty of experienced men, such as Scott McManus, Dale Probert, the Denny boys from Tanacross, (and their sister Nellie) as well as my old boss, Bill Mitchell, from whom to receive advice.

Tok hosts the 3rd most popular sprint race in Alaska each spring too; The Tok Race of Champions. Its most famous champion was a fella I once worked for, Gareth Wright. Gareth is known as the 'Father of the Aurora Husky', a specific breed of dogs which our kennel lines partially come from. It's amazing to think that he won the Tok race in 1953 and again in 1983— thirty years apart!

Much like Joe Redington, men with lifetimes filled with adventure and success are my greatest mushing heroes. This past season we created Tok's first long-distance event—The Top of The World 350.

Photo by Nicole Faille

This race runs between our town and the village of Eagle to the North some one-hundred-dred-and-seventy-five miles away. The trail we travel upon is the Taylor highway, which is not plowed in

the winter, allowing us endless miles of training op-
portunities. Much of this trail is hills with three major
mountains to cross over; training around here guaran-
tees a nice solid team of dogs each year that can compete with any of Alaska's best.

We have always wanted to create an event
here, and dedicated the inaugural race to Chief Isaac
Juneby from Eagle who passed away earlier in the
year. The Potts family, along with many others
helped to make sure that Isaac's name was honored
properly. The twenty-two mushers who participated
did their part—all of them finished with fine looking
dog teams! It was heartwarming to see a group of
people—many of whom travelled from Canada to
participate—come together as one, creating some
mushing magic for the rest of the world to enjoy.

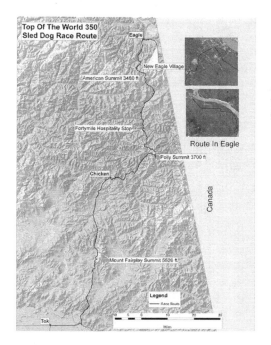

The 350 race was also a chance for us to show off the wondrous majesty of Alaska's eastern interior. A chance to help a native family heal, create something new for Tokites to enjoy following, and our musher friends to be a part of. This race will become even larger in years to come; numerous folks are already planning for next season's get together—a chance to celebrate our beloved home in the greatest way possible, by running dawgs in Alaska!

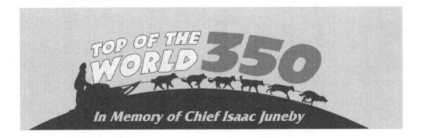

In my wildest dreams I never could have imagined all that these eyes have seen on this unique journey we have been on. Sunsets witnessed over American Summit while racing in the Quest, the exquisite beauty of Alaska's frozen arctic coastline as we push on into Nome in the Iditarod. The storms, the cold, frozen body parts; so many stories to be told. Yet to keep all of this knowledge to myself—our history of adventure in the northland—would be the most selfish thing to do. Having the opportunity to share some of our tales about the doggie's tails has been a rare treat, after all not too many kids are fortunate enough to have been able to pursue their dreams as I have been. Sure, there have been disappointments, heartaches and nightmares along the way but the opportunity to help others live vicariously through our adventures has always been a wonderful feeling. Through television and the internet people on all parts of our planet have been afforded the chance to not only follow dog mushing races more intensely but learn about dog mushers daily lifestyles as well. I've always taken great pride in not only our kennel's accomplishments but the longevity of our pooches' careers. My first leader, June-Mari, is still vibrant at the age of seventeen now, and her son Maestro is fourteen, each of these pooches has competed in over ten one thousand mile events. A 'younger' dog, like my boy Wally at the age of eight, has already competed in eight long-distance events. Adding up all of the mid-distance races we've been a part of each year one finds our annual amount of race miles averages over three thousand each winter. Add in the endless miles of training either by sled or four-wheeler and you can imagine that our pooches are some of the toughest, most well traveled animals on the planet!

Photo by Nicole Faille

What separates our Alaskan huskies though, is the size of their hearts; the love they share with us on a daily basis is breathtaking to behold. It's not just the hugs we share or the luscious licks of gratitude upon our faces but the opportunity to be a part of their world each day. Witnessing the interactions amongst the canines helps to create who we are too. Some folks choose to have overly disciplined dog yards but my hope has always been to create a pack where we are all equals on a common journey. We humans might be in charge of feeding and cleaning everyday but without mutual respect a dog team will never succeed in the long run. Often I've learned over the years to keep my mouth quiet instead of shouting out orders or commands all the time. Sometimes silence is one's greatest ally; sit back and let the dogs run the show! Delilah or Walter is just as capable of keeping the kids in line as I am. A happy whistle or humming a tune often will create a more positive atmosphere instead of telling everyone what to do all the time.

The beauty of being a true Dog-Man is that you always have more to learn, constantly tinkering with the team on the trail, seeking to create a prettier picture. One can get bored sometimes, however, if they choose not to travel different trails; after all, exploring new sights is what brought us up to Alaska in the first place. Mushing in the Greatland will always be a challenge; Mother Nature can never be taken for granted. My heart, however, will always yearn to explore other areas of this amazing earth of ours. Having the chance to view other cultures and environments by dog team is another dream come true, so this year we decided to mix it up a bit. Any of you kids want to play in Scandinavia?

The eight previous years our kennel had competed in the Yukon Quest in early February, taken a few weeks off then participated in the Iditarod, which begins the first weekend in March. Over the years we proved that dogs perform quite well in both races as they become more accustomed to travelling long spells on the trail. Modern day mushing is really about who has the best team, not the group of genetically enhanced dogs. It's the bond between human and dogs which creates overall success; knowing how fast to travel, rest, feed, etc.

This spring would be different.

After finishing 2nd in the Quest, I drove down to Anchorage and loaded up some dogs, with the help of my buddy Dave Scheer, into some airline kennels. It was time to explore!

After a brief layover in Chicago at my good friend Pat Moon's place, George, Jewel and Kotzebue joined me on the journey of a lifetime; we were heading for Stockholm, Sweden. Over the next few weeks we would be competing in three different events; the Amundsen 200, the Finnmarkslopet (700 miles) as well as the Beaver Trap Trail race. Mats Pettersson was my host, as well as his friend Taisto Torneus; they both reside in Kiruna, Sweden. Not only distinguished mushers, both men operate large tourism operations as well, showing thousands of Europeans the beauty of their dogs. Mats was kind enough to help me organize food drops for the races, find dogs to borrow, as well as a sled, compliments of Imel Inuan. I had hoped to bring more of my own pooches to race with, but considering the airlines charge $10,000 each way for just eight dogs, I opted to only bring a few leaders instead. Our first race took place in Sweden, the Amundsen 200, which is dedicated to famed polar explorer, Roald Amundsen. In the race to the South Pole, Roald had proven the efficiency of using dogs in wintertime travel. The Norwegians had been the first to the Pole while their English counterparts, lead by Robert Falcon Scott, refused to travel in this fashion and subsequently perished in the end.

There are two separate divisions for the Amundsen race, twelve and eight dog classes. Having only been in Europe for a few days I barely knew any of the dogs I was borrowing and decided to participate in the smaller class.

It was a wake-up call!

Fewer dogs meant more work for the musher but it was definitely an advantage having my main leaders, Jewel and her brother George, leading the way. Our team performed well in the rather warm twenty degree weather finishing in 3rd overall. The trails were relatively flat compared to a race like the Quest, and better groomed as well.

Competing against many mushers who barely spoke any English was fun too; informal sign language was often the main type of communication while out on the trail. Taisto's team won the event; considering he is one of the most gifted Dog-Men I've ever met, this was no sur-

Captain Roald Amundsen

prise. I was honored to be given the humanitarian award for best care of one's dog team; a coveted award for any musher to cherish. Taisto had previously helped Joe Redington when Joe had raced in the Lillehammer, Olympics in 1994. I was the first Alaskan to race in Scandinavia since then.

Taisto left me in awe with his stories of that year, he was even kind enough to let me wear Joe's Mitts which had Norwegian commands for 'gee' and 'haw' written on them in marker. Having the opportunity to represent Alaska was a very humbling feeling. For some of us just saying the word brings tears to our eyes. Alaska, you are my greatest love forever.

Fortunately we would have more time to prepare for the biggest race in Europe, Norway's Finnmarkslopet event. Though not as long as the Quest or Iditarod this race is just as challenging with endless hills, monstrous storms to deal with as well as some of the finest mushers in the world. Two-time Iditarod Champion Robert Sorlie was a main competitor, as well as Sigrid Ekran, Inger-Marie Halland, Thomas Waerner, and others.

Hera and George leading the way.

For this race I would once again have my two main leaders mixed with dogs borrowed from various kennels; Mats' as well as Svein Kartvedt's and Kjell Brennoden's. It would be a challenge, not only to finish the race, but communicate with dogs I had just met a few days before the event began! Luckily a few of these pooches were race veterans; knowing where you're going is always good whether one is human or canine. Like our earlier competition there would be two divisions; fourteen and eight dog classes, one-hundred-fifty teams total. Talk about a lot of energy on the trail!

This time we'd be playing with the bigger teams, hoping to not get lost if possible. Considering I could not even understand the trail signs in Norwegian, this scenario was more than likely. "Mr. Finnmarkslopet", Roger Dahl was kind enough to host us as well as my handler Juho Yllepsia. The race began in Alta and I immediately noticed how well orchestrated it was; huge banners and television monitors were everywhere. This was the most organized event I had ever seen. Norway's cultural beauty was every-

Mats Pettersson, Sven Engholm, Hugh, Taisto, Sami reindeer herder
Photo by Juho Yllepsia

where, not only the mushers, but Sami Natives as well.

I was asked to give a few presentations before the race but was relieved to finally get on the sled runners as we were off into the wilderness.

With so many teams running in rather warm temperatures, the trail was quite slow and punchy. We were in no hurry; this was the adventure of a lifetime! Unlike most events in Alaska mushers here are allowed to receive help from handlers at checkpoints, though the mushers were the only ones allowed to feed and care for their teams. Most of the other mushers had fancy dog trucks, campers or trailers where they were allowed to sleep and relax. Spending time with the dogs has always been more my style, there is always plenty of time to catch up on rest once the race is over.

Of Finnish decent, Juho was the best handler, as well as Svein, that I could ask for. Not only having

everything ready for me upon arrival, but letting me know details of the trail as he had competed in the area in previous years.

During the first half of the race we performed well in the stormy conditions, George and Jewel turned the team around a few times in the violent winds but we were lucky enough to be near local, seasoned mushers who helped

Photo by Christiane Ødegaard

guide us in the right direction. I made sure to give my Norwegian dog team lots of extra loving and massages knowing that they were just as confused as I was, "What language is this dude speaking?"

Nearing the halfway point in Kirkenes, we were now near the border with Russia.

Pulling into Kirkenes, I checked in, asking for a veterinarian so that I could drop one of the dogs who were too pooped out to continue on. Glancing around the staging area I realized that only two other teams were still there. We were in 15th place at this point so I decided to push on after a relatively short six hour run. All the spectators had smiles on their faces as we departed the downtown area, little did I realize the reason for this at the time.

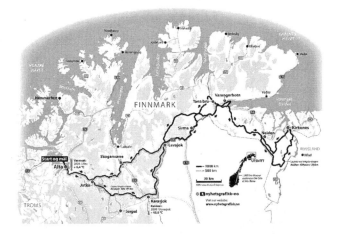

The Finnmark trail at this point of the race looped back around connecting with the Pasvik trail, returning us to Neiden. A few hours out from Kirkenes, as we traveled along the border of Finland, it began snowing lightly, which was nice considering that we were running during the middle of the day. I had a strange feeling that something was wrong though; the team was running fine but I had not seen anyone else in quite some time. Were we lost?

Later on that afternoon I finally spotted another human as a snow machine approached us. Stopping the team to let them by we had a brief conversation that left me laughing like a mad man.

Photo by Mina Sveen

"Hugh! You are now in the lead of the Finnmarkslopet race, how does it feel?

"Wh — wh — whaaat???"

Photo by Christiane Ødegaard

Unbeknownst to me there was another resting spot in Kirkenes where all of the teams were camped on the other side of a hotel. I was wondering why the trail seemed so clean of other dog tracks, now I had my answer!

"You, have got to be kidding me, my life is so weird." was my astonished reply.

Having snacked the team with some fish, I bid adieu to the cameramen as we

149

continued to the next resting area. I knew we would never be able to win against such stiff competition but having the opportunity to be in the front of such a historical event with a bunch of dogs that I had just met was victory in itself.

Half of the time while traveling I was repeating the pooches' names, trying to figure out which one matched which name. That afternoon, instead of sharing the trail with hordes of other mushers, we had the rare and lovely experience of being alone with nature. Isn't this what all mushers seek in the first place?

George and Jewel performed well but our team's main leader was a gal by the name of Hera, who I had borrowed from my buddy Svein.

Photo by Christiane Ødegaard

Most female dogs are a bit smaller on average than their male counterparts but not this lady; she towered over them. George looked like a Chihuahua next to Hera's seventy pound figure, she was not the fastest pooch in the team but Hera made up for it with her attitude. "Follow me kids, I've been here before, I'll show you which way to go."

Arriving that night back in Neiden, people were amazed at what we had done; perplexed that a rookie could be in the lead. Knowing we would need a longer rest I realized that our 1ˢᵗ place position would be short lived, but enjoyed the moment with friends nonetheless.

"Hugh people are saying that you blew through Kirkenes because you were afraid of the Russian border guards; is this true?"

"Not in the least, in fact I'm hoping to race in the Ural mountains or Lake Baikal in Siberia one day. I was just having some alone-time with the pooches. Is that ok?"

The frontrunners caught up a few hours later. I watched as people scrambled in every direction preparing their teams for the next leg of the journey. A team of veterinarians went over all of my dogs letting me know which pooches needed tending to or a little extra food. It was otherworldly to watch a group of professionals speaking a foreign language as they checked out the dogs. Too funny, what planet am I on? I felt like a kid in a candy store, to me this was the adventure of a lifetime.

It felt like being a rookie in the Quest or Iditarod all over again. Departing from Neiden, we were now in 5ᵗʰ place. I was following behind Trine

Photo by Christiane Ødegaard

151

Lyrek's team as we traveled northwest towards Varangerbotn. At this point in the competition, having traveled hundreds of miles in just a few days' time, all of the teams' overall speeds diminished. In long-distance racing this is when the musher needs to kick up their effort a notch with leg strength or by using their ski poles.

I had raced with Trine ten years ago in the Kobuk 440 when she was teamed up at Jeff King's kennel. Many of the top mushers are female in Scandinavia. Strength in our sport is not just muscles but the knowledge and determination that are in one's head too.

My team was not as fast as those in front of us but that didn't mean we were going to stop trying our best. Later that morning we saw a sign for Varangerbotn.

"Our next rest stop is just a few miles away kids!"

Crossing over a large area of frozen ice, another sign appeared:

YOU ARE NOW ON THE
ARCTIC OCEAN — BEWARE
OF SEALS ON THE TRAIL

"Holy cow!" I thought to myself. I had no idea we would be doing this — awesome. Varangerbotn was my buddy, Svein's, hometown and it was 152-beautiful; hundreds of fans with their children were waiting our arrival cheering us on.

After bedding down the dogs, we enjoyed some lunch consisting of reindeer stew. I decided to give the team a good rest in the heat of the day, the sun's rays had them snoozing away. There were only a few checkpoints left and I was becoming a bit sad, realizing that this beautiful journey would soon be finished.

Later that afternoon, we continued on. It's always difficult running in warmer temps, so I let my main girl Hera run solo up in front. Svein was as proud of her as I was. His smile was contagious keeping me in a positive mood. The trail was still quite demanding with numerous hills to pass over, a few of the faster more experienced teams passed by us, but this didn't matter.

What matters the most is how your team looks at the finish line!

Photo by Christiane Ødegaard

Eventual Champion Thomas Waerner, in his always cheerful voice exclaimed, "You're doing good Hugh!" He's a classy guy, which is what being a true champion is really about.

After the last major checkpoint, Skoganvarre, I gave everyone a few hours of extra rest in Jotka, knowing the other remaining teams were quite a ways behind. Temps the previous morning had plummeted to forty below, thus the day's sunshine was refreshing to all of us.

Late in the afternoon, as the outskirts of Alta came within our vision, tears trickled down my face knowing how well we had performed on this foreign soil. We might not have won, but folks will always tell the tale of that crazy fella from Alaska, wearing the Blue and Gold top hat, who knew how to put on a good show.
Helping others smile is what dog mushing is all about to me.

A large crowd awaited us at the finish line as loud music bellowed from some speakers. Trond Anderson, one of the Finnmarkslopet's organizers, presented me with our exquisite finisher's trophy as well as a prized Norwegian sweater. We might have been quite tired but my spirit was soaring up in the clouds.

"I promise you all that within a few years we will be back to race again—I LOVE Norway!"

It was time to enjoy a relaxing sauna.

At the ban-quet a few nights later I presented Robert Sorlie with a book about the Yukon Quest, invit-ing all the mushers to come try out our other Alaskan race

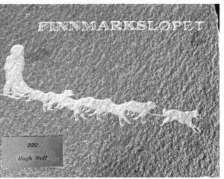

sometime soon. Whether it's the Quest, Finnmark, or Iditarod, all of these races are amazing in their own right. I laugh at those who try to compare them, or feel that one is better than the other. They are all quite unique from each other and deserve to have all the musher's respect. As if they were one of their dogs that should be cherished forever.

The next day one of the best mushers in Norway, Ralf Johanneson, presented me with a gift, "This is my Sami reindeer herding belt I want you to have it. Put it on your sled for good luck in future races!" Gestures such as this are priceless, Proof that the Heart of racing is in the dawgs, the people and the land.

Having raced in Norway, Canada, Australia, or just traveling throughout Germany or the United States; visiting with dog mushing enthusiasts makes one realize how huge this sport is around the world. Long-distance or sprint, people realize how amazing it is to be flying around Mother Nature with our beloved beasts leading the way. It has been such an honor to share my tails with many new found friends around the globe. By reading and enjoying our stories hopefully their spirits are energized to create a few more tales of their own. I have been racing for decades now, but at heart I'm just a kid; a nomadic Gypsy musher always in search of some lovely new tails to play with. Geronimo!

"Geronimo" by Mike Pickell

Photo by Ben Chang

Hugh was a Race Marshall in Australia in 2012.

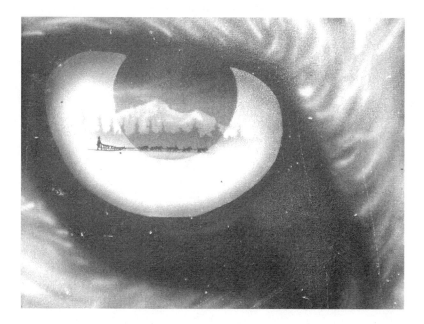

The Squaw Man
Robert Service

The cow-moose comes to water, and the beaver's
overbold,
The net is in the eddy of the stream;
The teepee stars the vivid sward with russet, red and
gold,
And in the velvet gloom the fire's a-gleam.
The night is ripe with quiet, rich with incense of the
pine;
From sanctuary lake I hear the loon;
The peaks are bright against the blue, and drenched
with sunset wine,
And like a silver bubble is the moon.

Cloud-high I climbed but yesterday; a hundred miles
around

I looked to see a rival fire a-gleam.
As in a crystal lens it lay, a land without a bound,
All lure, and virgin vastitude, and dream.
The great sky soared exultantly, the great earth bared
its breast,
All river-veined and patterned with the pine;
The heedless hordes of caribou were streaming to the
West,
A land of lustrous mystery – and mine.

Yea, mine to frame my Odyssey: Oh, little do they
know
My conquest and the kingdom that I keep!
The meadows of the musk-ox, where the laughing
grasses grow,
The rivers where the careless conies leap.
Beyond the silent Circle, where white men are fierce
and few,
I lord it, and I mock at man-made law;
Like a flame upon the water is my little light canoe,
And yonder in the fireglow is my squaw.

A squaw man! Yes, that's what I am; sneer at me if
you will.
I've gone the grilling pace that cannot last;
With bawdry, bridge and brandy – Oh, I've drank
enough to kill
A dozen such as you, but that is past.
I've swung round to my senses, found the place
where I belong;
The City made a madman out of me;
But here beyond the Circle, where there's neither
right or wrong,
I leap from life's straight-jacket, and I'm free.

Tails of the Gypsy Musher

H.H. Neff

Yet ever in the far forlorn, by trails of lone desire;
Yet ever in the dawn's white leer of hate;
Yet ever by the dripping kill, beside the drowsy fire,
There comes the fierce heart-hunger for a mate.
There comes the mad blood-clamour for a woman's
clinging hand,
Love-humid eyes, the velvet of a breast;
And so I sought the Bonnet-plumes, and chose from
out the band
The girl I thought the sweetest and the best.

O wistful women I have loved before my dark dis-
grace!
O women fair and rare in my home land!
Dear ladies, if I saw you now I'd turn away my face,
Then crawl to kiss your foot-prints in the sand!
And yet – that day the rifle jammed – a wounded
moose at bay –
A roar, a charge . . . I faced it with my knife:
A shot from out the willow-scrub, and there the mon-
ster lay. . . .
Yes, little Laughing Eyes, you saved my life.

The man must have the woman, and we're all brutes
more or less,
Since first the male ape shinned the family tree;
And yet I think I love her with a husband's tender-
ness,
And yet I know that she would die for me.
Oh, if I left you, Laughing Eyes, and nevermore came
back,
God help you, girl! I know what you would do. . . .

I see the lake wan in the moon, and from the shadow
black,
There drifts a little, *empty* birch canoe.

We're here beyond the Circle, where there's never
wrong nor right;
We aren't spliced according to the law;
But by the gods I hail you on this hushed and holy
night
As the mother of my children, and my squaw.
I see your little slender face set in the firelight glow;
I pray that I may never make it sad;
I hear you croon a baby song, all slumber-soft and
low –
God bless you, little Laughing Eyes! I'm glad.

Other Memories from the Trail

Hugh Neff, Jake Berkowitz, and Joar-Leifseth Olsom
Photo by Nicole Faille

Photo by Tracie Stalker

Photo by Tracie Stalker

Photo by Tracie Stalker

Photo by Tracie Stalker

Sui Kings and Hugh Neff   *Photo by Tracie Stalker*

Photo by Tracie Stalker

My handlers; Bruce Hagstrom, john "Fanman" Johnson, and
Jaime Vives

Photo by Tracie Stalker

Eagle Summit   *Photo by Tracie Stalker*

Yukon River   *Photo by Tamra Reynolds*

Photo by Tamra Reynolds

Hugh, Dick Ellsworth, Hobo Jim, and Lance Mackey.
Photo by Tamra Reynolds

Photo by Tamra Reynolds

Omen's offspring   *Photo by Tamra Reynolds*

Geronimo   *Photo by Tamra Reynolds*

Hugh with May Touk, President of the French Dog Mushing Association

Photo by Sui Kings

Photo by Nicole Faille

Photo by Nicole Faille

Photo by Christiane Ødegaard

Photo by Nicole Faille

"Life should not be a journey to the grave with the intention of arriving safely in a well preserved body, but rather to skid in broadside in a cloud of smoke, thoroughly used up, totally worn out and loudly proclaim, 'Wow! What a Ride!'" HST

Like us on Facebook at facebook.com/gypsymusher

Acknowledgements

When I arrived in Alaska with a few dogs and $200 to my name I really had no idea just how bizarre my life was about to become. My dream was never to win this race or that race; I just wanted to be a real dog musher, a true Alaskan. Lil' did I realize how difficult it would be to just survive. Over the years there have been some successes, but in order to slowly "move up the ladder of life" numerous souls have helped the Dream continue to progress. I would like to highlight a few of these folks as well as acknowledge as many folks as I can remember also.

The Laughing Eyes Kennel family is now worldwide with friends ranging from Koln, Germany to New South Wales, Australia, Sweden, Norway, Finland, of course The Greatland, as well as the 'lower 48 states; so many supporters of the beautiful beasts who are my family. Here are a few people who have been integral to our overall achievements these past seventeen years.

Tamra Reynolds was my kennel partner from 2004 until 2011, without her shared love of the dogs none of my recent achievements on the trail would have been possible. We shared some wonderful moments on Annie lake that I will always cherish, but my greatest love will always be Alaska. Tamra is still one of my best friends and I will always be thankful to have had her and her family in my life.

Richard Doran gave me a job and place to stay when I first moved to Fairbanks, also a former Chicagoan. As a Vietnam War veteran Rich gave me an even greater respect for those who have served our country proudly. Bill and Billie Mitchell hired me for my first handler job and are now my neighbors here in Tok.

The Erharts are like family; when I race I'm always seeking to make them proud. My native friends from all the interior villages: Minto, Manley Hot Springs, Nenana, Tanacross, Eagle, etc. have always made me feel good about where I live- Indian country.

Iditarod and Quest veteran Dave Scheer has been a great host over the years whenever I'm passing through Wasilla. Whether it be the Iditarod or my travels around the world Dave is one of the nicest people with tons of mushing insight; there's a reason I've been successful with friends like him.

Robert Forto, The Dog Doctor, has been invaluable as well. My co-host for the Gypsy Musher radio show hopes to compete in the Iditarod one day too, and I hope he does! In Fairbanks my friend, Sam Harrell, has always lent a hand. Whether it be food drops for races, or a place to keep the dogs before or after races Sam's kindness is well appreciated. Dawson Dolly aka Cindy Godbey, of Skagway, has been a wonderful character to share some hilarious times with too. Dolly personifies Alaska- wild with a warm heart, "Rolling, Rolling, Rolling down the river..."

My friend Ray Foxx from Nenana was also a godsend when I was going through some tough economic times. My buddies Bruce Hagstrom and John 'Fanman' Johnson have been great help as handlers over the last few years too. Jane Gennarro, my southern cook and good friend is one of the classiest ladies I know.

As far as veterinary help Eric Jayne was incredible in all he did for our dogs as well as thousands of others throughout the Greatland. His son Mike was my 1st Quest handler who was a great racer too. Renee Rember, Mercedes Eilleen, Clint Krusberg and many other vets have been helpful as well- thanks for all that you do!

During my time working in Coldfoot Northern Alaska Tour Company were great employers who were quite nice to let a worker keep twenty dogs on their property as well as give them time off so that they could compete in races.

Thanks to all of the folks in Skagway and Seward who were fun to hang out with in the summers when we were giving tour rides. Thanks to my friends in the mushing world too, you know who you are. Trying to have cordial relationships in such a competitive business can be a double edged sword. Over time one realizes that a smile and witty banter does not necessarily mean that people like you or say nice things about you when you're not around. Through the years I realized that judging others is a waste of time especially when my dogs are what life for me is all about.

I can be a very difficult person to be around at times so a personal shout out goes to all of those people who worked with me over the years. My Boy Scout buddies from Troop 31; Mike, Steve, Tim--it's an honor to have known you for all of these years since our grubby scout childhood days. I should also thank the woman who has been a special part of my life for the last few years, Nicole Faille, who shares with me a great love for playing with the dogs in the wilderness. Nic's gonna be a gifted dog musher in the future too. I barely beat her in this season' Kobuk 440 race just a few months ago.

In all of my travels, whether in Alaska or any where on this earth host friends and families have been lovely to visit with, especially folks like Sui Kings, Tracie Stalker, my teacher friends in North Carolina, New York and points in between. Of all my successes over the years besides the love of the dawgs newfound friends has been my greatest award. Love me or fear me, Laughing Eyes Kennel is here to stay and ready to play. More adventures are on the way, here's hoping that our story helps you to find your story, your way.

This book has been 10 years in the making, heaps of notes have been scattered about the cabin for years now—a 'huge mess'. Thanks to Nicole for helping me organize all of this. Summer Sea, another Alaskan author, is the creative genius who put it all together with her amazing talent and skills. Thanks to her as well as her husband Larry for putting up with the madness these past few months, Friends for life!

If there's one thing I've learned along the way it's this: By sharing with others, giving of yourself; life has special treasures to share with you too. I plan on giving all of my soul to Alaska and my extended family in the future- for this life is an adventure- we are all 1 LOVE.
Enjoy the View,
Hugh

Laughing Eyes Kennel Angels

Dave Sheer, Sam Harrel, Robert Forto, Sui Kings, Rainier Deinert, Annettchen Tobe, Konnie Fahl, Tracy Stalker, Harriett Jane Gennaro, Lisa Seifert, Cindy Godby "Dawson Dolly" , the Neff family, The Faille family, Bob Abbott, Pete Kanwischer, the Earhart family, Tom Denny, Nick Wirak, Jjay Levy, Dale Probert, Jim Ostry, Tamra Reynolds, Rich Doran, Christian Seidel, Pat Moon, Mats Petterson, Juho Yleppsia, John Larson "Fan Man" Johnson and family, Maggie & Damon Brooks, Mike Pickell, Louise Russell, Diane Johnson, Joanne Potts, The Redington Family, The Mackeys, John Lucas, Northern Alaska Tour Company, Wayne and Scarlet Hall, Bill and Billy Mitchell, Barb Angaiak, Ed Klem, Chris and Ida Peacock, Pat Barrett, Ray Fox, Dick and Joni Ellsworth "Ivory Jack's", Rick Hillman, Sally Young, Mike Williams, Joe Garnie, Bill and Brenda Borden, Aaron Burmeister, The Brooks Family, Mark Nordman, Bernie, Ingebrett, , Richard Doran, Jaime Vives, Benedikt Beisch, June Shelley, the Cadzow family, Don Kelly, the Peacock family, the Dempsey Woods family. the Klem family, Pat Barrett, G-pa Owens, Dawson City's El Dorado Hotel, Tawnee Knight, Marlys Sauer, Kevin Bodhi, Greg Heister, Jaime Schwartzwald, Amanda Simonson Price, Ernesto Nieves, Ken Huff, Larry Westlake, Laura Taylor, Virginia Brainerd, the Rotter family, the Brattrud family, Kev and Val Thain, VDB watches, GBA Carona, Petro North and all of our faithful sponsors, Delta Meat and Sausage, Mr. Lew Freedman and Alaska's Hobo Jim.

Where's my cowboy hat? It's time to dance...

Photographer's Pages:

Mark Gillette: https://www.facebook.com/Suitcase-Media

S.G.Sea: http://wrayvynn.deviantart.com/

Carol Falcetta: http://www.flickr.com/photos/ak-firebug

Scott Chesney: http://locolobo.zenfolio.com/

Susan Smalley-Stevenson: https://www.facebook.com/SusanLStevensonPhoto-graphy

Pat Kane: http://www.patkanephoto.com/